50
Great Investments
for the 21st Century

Diego J. Veitia

Dearborn
Financial Publishing, Inc.®

Also by Diego J. Veitia

Profit Potential in Global Emerging Markets
Strategic Metals: Its Uses and Investment Potentials

Executive Editor: Cynthia A. Zigmund
Managing Editor: Jack Kiburz
Interior Design: Professional Resources & Communications, Inc.
Cover Design: Rattray Design

©1997 by Diego J. Veitia

Published by Dearborn Financial Publishing, Inc.®

Printed in the United States of America

97 98 99 10 9 8 7 6 5 4 3 2 1

Library of Congress Cataloging-in-Publication Data

Veitia, Diego J.
    50 great investments for the 21st century / Diego J. Veitia.
      p. cm.
    Includes index.
    ISBN 0-7931-2480-8
    1. Investments—United States. 2. Twenty-first century.
  I. Title.
  HG4910.V43 1997   97-9140
  332.6—dc21   CIP

Dedication

This book is dedicated with much love to Dr. C. Castaneda, a true visionary and trendsetter.

Acknowledgments

Thanks to many good friends who have toiled endless hours with the making, remaking, editing, and reediting of this manuscript.

Albert Bloser
Jackie Briganti
Pat Garrard
Paula Grant
Aletta Harper
Jeff McKinley
Karen Morea
Steve Sjuggerud
Victoria Storm
Christopher Weber
Andrew West
Bill Young

Contents

Preface

You have never read a book like this. It doesn't predict the future like books that predict trends without showing how you can profit in a basic dollar-and-cents way. It doesn't tell you how to become rich like books that offer investment advice without helping you to understand how that advice follows logically from forecasted, general trends. This book does what these books don't do. It discusses trends and the specifics necessary to profit from them, and it shows you how to put these trends into a worldwide perspective.

Even though the world is changing at a dizzying pace, certain trends are emerging and the likelihood they will continue can be predicted with a high degree of certainty. This book not only looks at ten such trends, it helps you prepare for and prosper from them. Some of the trends leading to these changes are present now, but not many people see or understand them. Take the U.S. currency, for example. You may have heard how the dollar has periodically fallen against major European and Asian currencies. If you do not understand the causes for this trend or the chances that it will continue, you are also unlikely to understand how this trend can affect your financial investments. There is a chapter in this book that will show this to you.

My premise in this book is that anyone can learn to anticipate trends and identify the industries and companies that are likely to benefit from those trends. In a dollars-and-cents fashion, this book shows you how you can ride the wave of future trends. After reading it, even if you are hesitant to participate in the investment vehicles profiled, you will feel connected to the exciting changes happening around you. What you once found complicated and intimidating will become not only clear, but even part of your life.

I didn't write this book to be a source of "hot tips." Instead, I will show you how to approach the following ten trends that are propelling us into the future. In each chapter, I first identify a trend and then discuss specific characteristics to look for when deciding which companies are likely to benefit from that trend.

The Ten Trends

1. The Growing Global Marketplace Trend

As the world's economy grows larger, the U.S. share of it is becoming smaller. More and more, the fastest growing stocks, the highest yielding bonds, and certificates of deposit are turning up not in the United States, but overseas. To prosper in the future, investors need to know how to expand their horizons and invest internationally.

2. The Falling Dollar Trend

As the U.S. dollar loses value against currencies of countries better able to produce goods and provide services, and as the U.S. manufacturing base shifts to other parts of the world, there will be winners and losers. Among the distinct beneficiaries will be investors able to capitalize on the better returns available in stronger instruments outside the U.S. dollar.

3. The Pre-Emerging Markets Trend

In the rapidly shifting global economy, there are big players, small players, and those that are striving just to become players. Players in the last category are the last frontier of investment opportunities—and for investors willing to brave this frontier, the adventure may be risky but rewarding.

4. The Manufacturing Trend

The world's manufacturing base is shifting fast. A generation or so ago, the United States was home to that base, but no longer. Now it has moved to other parts of the world. The companies perfectly placed to take advantage of this shift are not U.S. companies. They are from countries with booming economies, and investing in the best of them will be a must for future prosperity.

5. The Telecommunications Trend

Asia, Latin America, and parts of Europe are bursting with growth. Even so, they lack much of the telecommunications infrastructure that Americans take for granted. The companies in the forefront of this growth are exciting and potentially lucrative investment vehicles.

6. The Education Trend

America is falling behind in teaching basic education skills. This trend must be reversed or we will soon be unable to compete in the global arena. As the country moves to remedy this problem, companies involved in education will benefit greatly from technological advances in the field.

7. The Entertainment Trend

The American entertainment industry is one of the few U.S. industries that triumphs over all foreign competition. As technological advances in this industry continue to astound the world, the purveyors of this technology will be exciting companies to watch and to invest in.

8. The Environmental Trend

This trend has a positive and a negative side for companies and their investors. As concern for the environment intensifies, government regulations are nurturing some companies while crippling or destroying others. Picking the winners involves looking at both sides of the trend.

9. The Personal Security Trend

As many Americans watch their standard of living fall and many others sink into poverty, crime will increase, as will the demand for personal security. Companies that satisfy this demand are ones to watch.

10. The Biotechnology Trend

Whether it's curing diseases or growing better vegetables, biotechnology companies are making advances that will bene-fit billions worldwide. Buying stock in the companies on the leading edge of this industry is investing in companies that are helping to shape our future quality of life.

Despite the successful track record I've created while building my investment firm to a major presence in global markets, I know that it is impossible to predict precisely what the future has in store. Though my thinking on some of the specific companies mentioned may change, I believe the basic trends I discuss in this book will remain intact. For now, read and enjoy this book. If what I say makes sense, you can con-sider further action.

We live in one of the most exciting times in history, and changes are all around us. Those who prepare for these changes and take action will thrive. I hope you will be among them.

—Diego J. Veitia

The Dawn of the New Millennium

The End of the Industrial Revolution, the Birth of the Technological Age

Once every 200 or 300 years, cultural, political, and economic changes seem to quicken their pace and radically alter the face of the world. During times like these, it is common for those who live through and witness such radical transformation to no longer remember the world of their youth. For instance, a teenager living in Russia today will have only faint memories of the Soviet home in which he was born, and it is still likely that the face of his Motherland will transform many times before his death. In the case of the fall of the Communist Empire, the extreme sudden collapse resulted from decades of gradual internal economic, cultural, and political deterioration.

Today, we look upon the events that led to the Soviet collapse with an understanding of the underlying trend, failing Communism, that ultimately caused it. We could even say that the fall of Communism was predictable given the circumstances. Political revolution is one of the most abrupt forms of change that affects the economy and the people of our world. Other forms, such as cultural and economic trends, may be far more gradual and difficult to recognize but may produce similar effects.

New Global Trends Emerge

In the past century, technological advances have vaulted our world forward at a staggering rate. As we continue to invent better technology and as the world continues to grow and change, certain trends emerge. The likelihood that these patterns will continue can be predicted with a high degree of certainty and therefore can serve as a tool for smart investing.

In the 1950s, the introduction of the hula hoop redefined the American toy standard. Into the mainstream spun a large, round, colorful tube that revolutionized our idea of fun by incorporating music, exercise, dance, and plastic. Investors who saw only the fad bought into the toy companies that made the hula hoop and profited during the rage. However, those who recognized the trend and invested in the plastics industry profited long after the hula hoop fizzled out. In other words, the ability to differentiate between fads and trends will arm the investor with a powerful arsenal poised for profit. As we approach the 21st century, four major global trends are developing.

The End of the Industrial Revolution

First, and most significant, is the end of the Industrial Revolution as we have known it. The bulk of the world's manufacturing base, safely rooted in the United States since the late 19th century, is now leaving. As once dormant economies emerge, such as those in Asia, and offer lower costs to companies needing their services, their factories grow and produce goods so inexpensively that U. S. manufacturers cannot compete.

The New Technological Revolution

Second, as the most significant economic trend of this century comes to an end, a new and more powerful one is emerging: the technological revolution. The United States is by far the leader in this field, especially in the development of cutting-edge hardware and software, but the demand for technology in emerging economies is greater than ever, as they recognize the importance of communicating quickly and efficiently in a global economy.

Role of the Small Players

Third, the logical result of a global economy is the emergence of many small players whose role as a unit becomes extremely significant. For example, in the United States in the past several years, the major corporations have been downsizing and thus their employment roles have been shrinking. The smaller entrepreneurial companies have become the backbone of the economic and employment growth. (The U.S. Commerce Department indicates that a staggering 90 percent of non-government employment growth in the past five years is attributable to the smaller companies.) In areas such as Asia, Latin America, and Eastern Europe, where economies have traditionally been small by comparison to that of the United States, the global industrial shift and the availability of new technology has opened up many avenues for growth. As these economies grow, they make room for even smaller ones to enter the game. Pre-emerging markets can be found in some countries of Africa, for example, in which infrastructure is in the works and rich minerals are yet to be unearthed. In these economies, investment carries high risk but also the potential of high reward.

As smaller markets grow and contribute more to the world's industrial economy, U.S. participation inevitably decreases. In response to its inability to compete and its reluctance to shift to its present relative comparative advantage, technology, the U.S. trade deficit has mushroomed and caused the U.S. currency to suffer substantially. For instance, in 1972, a Swiss Toblerone chocolate bar cost an American 25 cents or one Swiss franc. To buy the same chocolate bar late last year, the American had to spend 80 cents. Incredibly, the price in Swiss francs has not changed in 25 years; it is still one Swiss franc. As the U.S. dollar loses value, as it has in the past 25 years, investors who benefit most will be those who are able to capitalize on better returns available in stronger currencies, like the Swiss franc, the German mark, or the Japanese yen.

A Response to America's Social and Moral Decay

Finally, a cultural trend is developing in response to the social and moral decay that cripples Americans with fear and anger and leaves them searching for protection and a higher quality of life. In the February 6, 1995, issue of *Newsweek,* an article by Jonathan Alter and Pat Wingert addresses "The Return of Shame" in America as its citizens rise against tolerance of crime and hope for the rebirth of a national moral conscience. Whereas our country is about "shamelessness," contest Alter and Wingert, Japan is about "shame . . . . But just when shame seems . . . dead [in the U.S.], red faces have begun to shove themselves back into our late-20th-century consciousness." The faces are those of our anger toward criminals and politicians as well as the one we'd like to see—the guilty feeling remorse.

To protect themselves against crime, Americans are investing in personal security systems and other similar products that might reduce their chances of being victimized. Like the hula hoop scenario, those who identify the trend and invest in the companies that heed the demand for personal security have the potential for generous profit.

On a much deeper level, the root of many social and economic problems in the United States is the inability of our schools to properly educate our students and to prepare them for a competitive job market. Procter & Gamble recently aired a television commercial illustrating the performance of U. S. students versus those of other nations in standardized tests. The American girl ranked 12th among her international peers and sent a shocking message to viewers: we are no longer competitive in education. As the country moves to remedy this situation, companies involved in education, especially those that seek to revolutionize teaching and ease learning, will benefit tremendously. Advances in educational technology make this area especially exciting to watch.

Factors included in other cultural trends, such as our attitudes about the environment and entertainment, are also affected by the conscience of America. As we slowly realize that we are responsible for the fate of our children, our nation, and ourselves, we consider the consequences of dumping hazardous materials into our water supply or of allowing our children to watch mindless television programs that brazenly parade sex, violence, and destruction. Fortunately, technological advances allow us to rectify pollution problems and have created a new niche in which smart investors can profit. Also, exciting computer systems will eventually enable us to choose our entertainment instead of letting the networks dictate our programming. Again, as we follow this trend, winning companies will surface and wise investments can be made.

Trends and the Investor

To an investor, the ability to identify trends and distinguish them from fads is a powerful and potentially profitable asset. However, the most valuable asset is patience. Often, investors are motivated by fear and greed and therefore neglect to monitor trends carefully. Instead, they rely heavily on messages from those hoping to profit from their ignorance. For example, the insurance companies in America prey on the fear that the family's only wage earner suddenly disappears or that a potentially fatal medical emergency occurs. While these events could happen and should be addressed in the investment decision-making process, fear, the emotion driving the decision, should be eliminated. Investors should instead focus on the odds of such calamities happening, on whether existing assets can be protected, on how future income needs can be calculated now with the assurance that those needs will be met, and most important, on whether or not the protection is really needed.

On the other hand, the greed-motivated investor, the one who spots an opportunity based in a tip, a rumor, or media hype and seizes it without exercising proper diligence, also falls prey to an emotion-driven market. In fact, an investor receiving a tip should seek more information about price-earning ratios, growth, earning trends, industry trends, capability of management, and so on in order to choose wisely.

Just as if we were waiting for a train, so too should we wait for the right investment. For surely, if we miss the 3:30, the Metroliner might be following close behind ready to carry us to our destination much more quickly and efficiently.

Principles of Long-Term Investing

Buy When Others Sell, Sell When Others Buy

What is it that really separates the great investors from the crowd? What allows them to consistently outperform the rest of Wall Street year after year? Is it luck? Is it brains? Or is it something else, something more? It's something more. The difference is that the great investors have a well defined and focused investment philosophy, coupled with a globally diversified approach to investing. That is it. No crystal balls or special computer programs are needed. It is philosophy and global diversification that allows the great investors to separate themselves from the crowd. The great investors are confident that, if they follow the rules and only invest when "all of the pieces fit," they will win over the long-term.

A Framework for Building Confidence

Winning in financial markets is as much or more a state of mind as it is hard analysis. You cannot consistently win unless you have the proper mental attitude. In an effort to infuse your

7

mental state with the "right" kind of thought, we offer this investor's pledge: "From this moment forward, I pledge that I will not make an investment unless I can do so with confidence." The entire process of developing confidence in an investment means that you have done your homework and the pieces fit. Following are four major elements that can help to inspire investment confidence:

1. *Know your reasons.* Always keep in mind your reason for making an investment. If your reasons are no longer valid, get out of the position, no matter what.

2. *Know your risk.* You will win some and lose some; that is a given when you participate in financial markets. Before you make an investment, always know how much you are willing to risk.

3. *Know your time frame.* Trade for a reason, but know that adverse price fluctuations can challenge your reasoning. Establishing a time-horizon will help distinguish those fluctuations that are random from those that challenge your rationale.

4. *Know yourself.* This is probably the hardest part. Do you really want to win in financial markets? How much risk can you handle? Can you cut your losses? Do you tend to be early or late when you invest in an idea? You must first know who you are before you can consistently take profits from the market.

To sum it up, your reason for making an investment dictates your time frame; the size of your investment is dictated by the risk you can handle.

It is the continuous fluctuations in financial markets that subject investors to the emotions of fear and greed—the means by which the market takes their money away. Because losses are sustained by those who succumb to their emotions, confidence is the key to developing a successful long-term investment philosophy.

Most likely, at one time or another, you have been "tricked" out of a winning investment position by the market. It was probably because of an adverse price fluctuation or following the advice of an "expert." You have probably also had the experience of making an investment, forgetting about it, then later learning that the investment ended up doing very well. You owned it for the right reasons, and you weren't tricked out of the position for the wrong reasons.

Axioms from a Legend

Arguably Sir John Templeton is one of the greatest investors the world has ever known. What is it that has allowed Sir John to consistently outperform some of the best money managers in the investment world? Sir John would probably say that his faith and disciplined investment philosophy were the keys to his success. Over the years, Sir John has developed several investment axioms, several of which follow:

- For all long-term investors, there is only one objective—"maximum total real return after taxes."
- Achieving a good record takes much study and work, and is a lot harder than most people think.
- It is impossible to produce a superior performance unless you do something different from the majority.
- The time of maximum pessimism is the best time to buy, and the time of maximum optimism is the best time to sell.
- To buy when others are despondently selling and to sell when others are greedily buying requires the greatest fortitude, even while offering the greatest reward.
- In the long run, the stock market indexes fluctuate around the long-term upward trend of earnings per share.
- In free-enterprise nations, the earnings on stock market indexes fluctuate around the replacement book value of the shares of the index.
- The time to buy a security is when the short-term owners have finished their selling, and the time to sell a stock is often when short-term owners have finished their buying.
- Too many investors focus on *outlook* and *trend*. Therefore, more profit is made by focusing on value.

- If you search worldwide, you will find more bargains and better bargains than by studying only one nation. Also, you gain the safety of diversification.

Granted, we cannot all expect to become John Templetons of the investment world. But we can learn a great deal from Sir John's axioms that will help us become better investors. It takes a great deal of confidence to "buy when others are despondently selling." How many of us were buying stocks in the midst of the Chinese Tienamen Square massacre during the summer of 1989? How many of us were looking for bargains on the day the U.S. stock market crashed on October 19, 1987? I would venture to guess very few of us. But we can probably assume that John Templeton and other great investors were buying during these times. They did their homework, had confidence in their investment philosophy, and understood the advantages of global diversification.

Global Diversification: Lower Risk and Enhance Return

If you search worldwide, you will find more bargains and better bargains than by studying only one nation. Also, you gain the safety of diversification.

—Sir John Templeton

The fact is that the world has become a global village and global investing makes sense as part of a balanced portfolio. An event 100 years ago that might have taken days to affect the world's economies now rushes around the world with lightning speed. Computers track markets constantly and detect the slightest fluctuations. What happens on Wall Street can affect markets in Tokyo, Bonn, and Sydney almost instantly. What happens in Singapore, Hong Kong, or London can push up or pull down the value of investments around the world. Investments everywhere are interconnected in a complex web of buying and selling that doesn't recognize the boundaries of countries. Domestic investors—whether they realize it or not—are impacted daily by global events. By diversifying internationally, an investor can harness the benefits of these events while reducing his or her risks.

Put Your Eggs into International Baskets

The most fundamental principle investors learn is not to keep all their eggs in one basket. These days that means not keeping them in any one company or one industry—or in one country. Spreading assets over different stock markets has shown to not only increase performance, but reduce risk at the same time.

The following chart may look a bit odd at first glance, but it tells a powerful story. It shows that a portfolio of 70 per cent U.S. and 30 percent international stocks not only produces a greater return than a portfolio of 100 percent U.S. stocks, but does so with less risk.

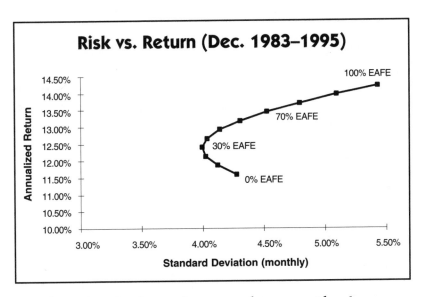

This risk reduction and return enhancement has been possible because of an imperfect correlation between the U.S. market and international markets. This means that even though what happens in one market can affect another, markets tend to move independently of one another. There are a number of reasons this happens, including: divergent business cycles, politics, and various structural differences. The imperfect correlation allows for gains from diversification. Seldom, for example, will the U.S., European, and Japanese markets move in tandem for any long period of time. Mark Hulbert recently wrote, "It looks like investment alchemy: lower risk by investing in a riskier asset. It isn't alchemy. It's just the logic of diversification."

Exciting Opportunities and Improved Performance

To limit yourself to merely investing in one country means greatly limiting your investment opportunities. International diversification provides a variety of potentially high-growth investment choices in stocks and bonds that are located in some of the best performing markets in the world.

If an investor chooses to invest only in domestic companies, he denies himself the opportunity of investing in some of the world's leading companies. The distinctions between companies and countries are blurring. The global market is here. The astute investor realizes this and is taking advantage of it.

By limiting a portfolio to U.S. stocks, an investor would have to ignore:

- ten of the ten largest construction and housing companies
- ten of the ten largest banking companies
- eight of the ten largest chemical companies
- eight of the ten largest machinery and engineering companies
- seven of the ten largest automobile companies

Source: Morgan Stanley Capital International and Templeton Funds

Just as companies do not prosper uniformly, nor do countries. Often, countries other than the United States are home to a few world-class competitive industries. By not venturing beyond the U.S. borders, it may be impossible to gain access to the best company in a given industry.

Country	World-Class Industries
Switzerland	Insurance Pharmaceutical Food Machinery
Germany	Chemical Automotive
Britain	Media-related business Motors
Australia	Mining Agriculture
Philippines	Accounting services Brewing
Sweden	Paper containers Power generation
Japan	Office equipment Automobiles Consumer electronics

The Global Village Awaits

The countries of the world are truly becoming interlinked as information technology brings us all closer together. It is a world that offers significant investment opportunity. But, to tap into this world, an investor must be willing to diversify internationally. It should be an easy decision. You now know that, by diversifying abroad, you will most likely increase your return, while at the same time reduce your overall risks. Simply put, with the proper guidance, investing internationally is the best single way to preserve and enhance your wealth.

You Can Do It

Many of us only dream of multiplying our money ten times on an investment. Why do we often settle for singles and doubles, when with a little effort, we could hit investment home runs? A long-term investment philosophy is almost a prerequisite to hitting the home runs we dream of. You may be surprised to see just how "lucky" you become once you begin to search the globe for the best values and only invest with confidence.

Winning in financial markets is not easy. It takes hard work and lots of study, but you can do it. As your confidence in your methodology builds, you develop your own investment philosophy—an investment philosophy that is suited for you. Your efforts will be rewarded by superior investment performance, and you will be able to separate yourself from the crowd.

Investing in Companies That Are Teaching Our Kids

The Education Trend

One of the most certain predictions about future trends is that more effort will be put into American education over the next generation than has been in the past. Among the reasons for this emerging trend is the shift in value placed on our children's importance in society. From the late 1960s to the mid-1980s, the greed-motivated "Me Generation" did not place any emphasis on children and their position as America's future leaders. These tendencies toward self-indulgence and greed were somehow encouraged and supported by popular culture as they had never been before. Fortunately, that overwhelming self-serving priority is changing as more and more people witness its negative influence on our youth. Staggering numbers of children are victims of drug abuse, poverty, physical abuse, and neglect largely because of the lack of responsibility among parents and society. Finally, however, all factions recognize an urgent obligation to reverse the conditions that led to such degeneracy in order to preserve and nurture our culture.

Baby Boomers Shift Focus

One reason for this change is that baby boomers have grown up and are having children of their own. As they do, they are shifting their focus from themselves toward their progeny. Sensing that standards of living are falling and recognizing how important education will be for their children's success and happiness, they are determined to give their children any possible "edge." If such a positive shift in attitude and motivation continues, it should have a profound effect on our students.

For, although our university system is the best in the world, our educational standards and test results, when compared to the rest of the developed world, have taken a nose dive over the past generation. Increasing numbers of American high school graduates are being edged out for the best opportunities by bright foreigners whose societies have emphasized the importance of education more than ours. Even after America's youth have gone through 12 to 16 years of schooling, they often can't compete with challengers from other countries.

This situation mirrors the competitiveness of many U.S. products of the past generation, which also have not been able to compete in the world marketplace. There is a direct connection between poor educational skills and a failing economy like ours; as they recognize this connection, it is apparent that Americans are willing to make the sacrifices necessary to rectify such an intolerable, pathetic situation.

Computers Provide Connection

Computers hold the key to transforming our nation back into an educational leader. Some players are in position to further capitalize on the software that has and will continue to have a positive impact on students. Technology that introduces our children to information through computers, CD-ROMs, and interactive television is filtering into millions of homes and many schools, and is helping to encourage and enhance a learning revolution. Computers can now serve as a link between home and school and subtly reinforce the importance of that educational connection.

Edutainment Software Programs Make Their Mark

The most poignant question facing the innovative technological leaders of the education revolution is how to keep students entertained and challenged so that they enjoy learning. In a brilliant response to this dilemma, the *edutainment* industry was born out of a marriage between entertainment and education, and has successfully made its mark on the computer world. Developments of edutainment software and programming have prompted many families to buy home computers so their children can develop skills previously confined to the classroom.

Even kids as young as three and four years old can use a new computer software game called Mickey's ABCs, which teaches children safety tips, musical culture, and the alphabet through simple commands. When turned on, the screen shows Mickey Mouse asleep. If the user presses "V" on the keyboard, Mickey wakes up and starts to play his violin. If "Q" is pressed, Mickey opens an oven, but if he gets too close he gets singed. Best of all, Mickey's activities are carried out with appropriate sound effects and speech so that the child truly interacts with him.

Another software package, Reader Rabbit, designed for the same age group also teaches the alphabet. With Reader Rabbit, a take-off on Roger Rabbit, the rabbit shows pictures of three different objects: a pig, a fox, and a bug, for example. As the letters naming each object appear jumbled at the bottom of the screen, Reader Rabbit helps kids unscramble them to spell out the name for each object.

Moving up the age ladder, the Carmen Sandiego series is one that makes the intellectual challenge more difficult. Based on the TV series, this computer software program is truly interactive and makes learning geography fun. Carmen is a notorious thief who jet-sets around the globe in a futile effort to escape justice. Kids must find where she is at each step by looking up answers to a broad range of geography questions that appear on the screen. Another software program, Math Blaster, hones in on kids' math skills. Blaster puts its users in an intergalactic shoot-out, where, to play well, the ability to solve math problems is as important as shooting accurately.

Especially resourceful to any student is Compton's Interactive Encyclopedia, which can be used to research all subjects. Its information is not restricted to written type, but is also relayed through compact disc-quality sound, animation, and even television or movie bits. The encyclopedia's arsenal features highlights such as the works of Shakespeare read aloud by noted actors, the high-quality music of great composers and visual reproductions of famous paintings. Students who have access to this program are treated to a technological array of information.

Virtual reality has also penetrated the edutainment library. In one program, The Body Illustrated, students of biology are shown with great detail how the human body functions. They witness how the muscular system works and how blood is pumped from the heart; they even see the heart pumping in a "virtual heartbeat." Another approach to virtual reality using computers is Knowledge Adventure, Inc.'s series of programs, which allow students to explore environments like the human body, the undersea world, and the world of dinosaurs, as if they were actually there.

The "here-and-now" world kids are growing up in is receiving interactive attention, too. The Maxis company sells a series of simulated real-world problem-solving programs such as Sim City, which allows kids to lay out their own city, balancing industry, homes, parks, fire departments, police, etc. Through trial and error, they learn that balanced budgets, low taxes, and a happy electorate are the ideal combination. They learn that if they make taxes too high, voters kick them out. If they make taxes too low, the program says they can't pay for police and garbage collection. Sim City was designed with adults in mind, but it has become a bigger hit with teenagers.

The idea behind most of these programs is to make learning so enjoyable that kids find it as entertaining as watching television. But not all edutainment software programs stress education. Some try to balance education and entertainment; others go just for the fun. For example, Humongous Entertainment of Woodinville, Washington, puts out programs such as Putt-Putt Goes to the Moon to teach critical thinking and problem solving to three to eight-year-olds. What it also does is to help kids have a good time without watching mindless and violent television programs. Humongous's products and approach mirror the background of its founders who offer a primary example of the power behind an education/entertainment combination. Until starting the company in 1992, they worked for LucasArts Entertainment (George Lucas's company) and made such movies as Star Wars and Indiana Jones.

Small Software Companies Impact Edutainment

Perhaps the most impressive impact of the edutainment industry can be seen in the success of small software companies that cater to educational programming. Until its recent takeover by CUC International, Davidson and Associates was the largest independent producer of edutainment software programs, with 1995 revenues of $147 million. Davidson and Associates, the makers of the Math Blaster program, was founded by Joy Davidson, a school teacher of 12 years who began writing computer programs to drill her students on vocabulary and math. Soon thereafter, she became her own publisher and with a $3,000 initial investment, created a company that grew modestly for ten years. Then, in 1992, the educational reform trends kicked in and gave rise to the demand for good edutainment products. As a result, Joy and her husband-partner took their company public in April 1993, turning a $3,000 investment into nearly $700 million.

As the Davidson example illustrates, the edutainment industry is growing extraordinarily quickly, and other companies like it are waiting for their turn.

Corporations Offer Edutainment Products

Large corporations in related entertainment areas have also seen how lucrative it is to create edutainment products, and they have invested much time and money in creating their own internal divisions. For example, Microsoft and Nintendo are each trying to set up areas expressly for edutainment, but it is unclear how successful they will be. Unfortunately, it is not an easy task and experience has shown that the truly creative and effective educational software products are more apt to come from small organizations, like Davidson and Associates, that interact with and respond directly to the children. Only time will tell what happens to the creativity of these companies as they become big and successful.

Broderbund Software

A company with a path similar to Davidson and Associates' is Broderbund Software. Started in 1980 by two brothers, its annual revenues had grown to nearly $186 million by 1996. Unlike Davidson, the company has yet to be bought out. Broderbund does, however, fit the profile of a company that could be bought out by a larger, want-to-be player needing to fill a creative void. For, as high as the stock price may be for a good company in a growing market, nothing compares to its stock price when the company is being sought and is ultimately bought.

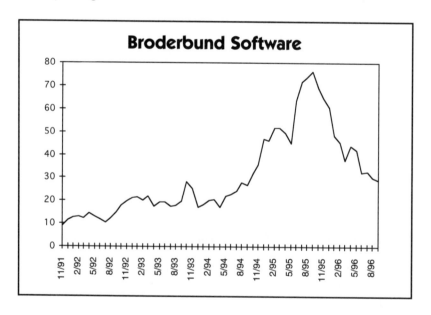

Much of the success of small software companies relies heavily on the purchasing power of the American family, since most public school funding does not allow for extravagant computer expenditures. If the public school arena opens to new technology, however, the results both in business and in education will be astounding.

Scholastic Corporation

One company that appears to be positioned to prosper from any scenario, however, is Scholastic Corporation. Since 1920, it has supplied children in classrooms with newsletters, magazines, and books. It also publishes books kids love to read outside of school. The most popular is the phenomenally successful Baby Sitter's Club series. Scholastic is, in fact, the English-speaking world's number one publisher and distributor of children's books. Scholastic is also involved in new technology, and its historical presence in the classroom enables it to sell software. Although its video and software sales amount to just 4 percent of total sales, they are likely to be the fastest growing. Scholastic was taken public in 1992.

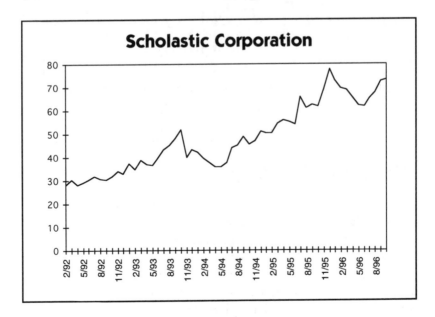

Harcourt General

Another company to watch is Harcourt General. The company owns nearly 1,500 cinemas in 31 states and controls the Neiman Marcus and Bergdorf Goodman retail stores, as well as other specialty apparel, jewelry, and home furnishing outlets. Despite the fact that Harcourt General is intent on acquiring promising software makers, the most exciting aspect of the company in terms of its edutainment interests is its publishing arm, the recently acquired Harcourt-Brace-Jovanovich. Harcourt has already been buying, as subsidiaries, many of the brightest edutainment software makers around.

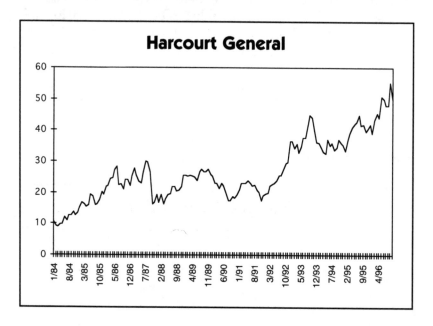

Informatics Holdings

In Singapore, as in most ethnically Chinese communities, the family places great importance upon education. The Singapore government also encourages all citizens to involve themselves in learning the technology of the 21st century.

The government of Singapore is actively involved in the development of Information Technology (IT) into the 21st century through a national IT plan. The goal of this plan is to transform Singapore from a low-tech manufacturing center to a high-tech manufacturing center and regional hub for commerce, communications, and transportation.

The government has developed the IT 2000 plan with a goal of making Singapore an advanced technology country by the turn of the century. IT 2000 is the development of a well integrated and extensive national information infrastructure (NII) based on advanced technology. This plan is going to be accomplished by looking at seven building blocks. These include IT manpower, IT culture, information communication infrastructure, IT applications, IT industry, climate for creativity and entrepreneurship, and coordination and cooperation. The IT 2000 master plan was developed after an exhaustive study led by the National Computer Board (NCB) along with a partnership including more than 200 senior executives from 11 major economic sectors in Singapore.

The approach that Singapore has taken was one of the first in the world and because of its importance, many other countries have begun to take the same approach. The government of Singapore also funds major research and development IT activities at universities, polytechnics, and within industry to help speed up the development of the country's technology base.

One company has discovered a way to make money by teaching technology to these very willing students. Established in 1983, Informatics Holdings Limited operates computer training schools and franchises for computer training. The company operates under the name "Informatics Computer School" and "Informatics Center for Advanced Seminars." Through its subsidiaries, the company is also engaged in the distribution of computers and related accessories, operation of computer training schools, publishing and distribution of educational magazines, provision of management services in operation of computer training schools, advertising agency, the operation of child development centers, provision of computer courses, and educational and business management consulting services.

The company has expanded beyond Singapore, establishing a chain of 123 computer training centers in more than 20 countries under a franchise program. Under this program, Informatics plans to open 200 by the year 2000. From these franchises, Informatics receives a S$300,000 franchise fee, and collects 5 percent of gross revenues. Additionally, the company is expanding into two new franchise concepts: a computer-assisted learning center, which will offer IT-assisted training for children, and a business training school.

As Singapore supports schools that teach its students to use the technology of the 21st century, other countries in Asia already see the success and seek to emulate it, suggesting that Informatics should find many eager customers throughout the region, where its expansion plans are directed

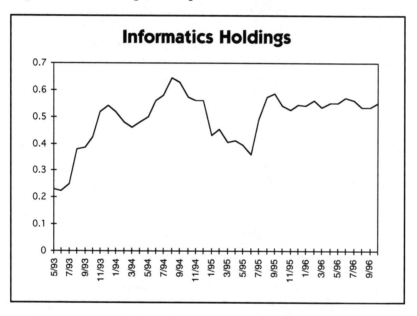

Computer Software Can Revolutionize Learning

Parents are ultimately responsible for providing their children with an education, primarily at home but also at school. Those who actively accept their duty and participate in their children's learning, especially from a young age, make an invaluable lasting impression on them. Both parents and teachers must unite to rebuild the American educational system; the burden cannot be placed on one or the other. Bureaucratic administrators cannot be expected to undo the mess, for they have the least contact with the children and do not have the ability to accurately respond to their needs.

There is alarming resistance from the present educational establishment to advances in computer software that can revolutionize learning. The greatest problems with these advances are that they challenge the current status quo by introducing new teaching methods, requiring teachers to use computers, and requiring schools to purchase computers.

Conventional teaching methods have been unable to stop the decline in children's performance levels, especially in the area of writing skills. Improved results have been achieved by using computer programs that take children through the writing process and then print out what they have written. When they see the fruits of their labor, the kids take pride in their accomplishments and are motivated to write more and write better.

Hopefully, most if not all the educational programming will have similar long-term effects. If used properly, these computers would make old teaching methods obsolete. Instead of learning according to the pace and program of the instructor, students could progress according to their own abilities, and become the center of their own learning while the teacher becomes a coach. The presence of computer programs like these in all American classrooms is necessary, if we want to raise the levels and standards of our educational system. Unfortunately, the shocking reality is that it is easier to get funding for security guards and metal detectors in public schools than for computers. Without the opportunity to use this technology, teachers and students will suffer and the recovery of the educational system will be thwarted.

As an investor, you can buy stocks directly in these new companies, such as Broderbund, or you can buy shares in larger companies with growing stakes in the field, such as Harcourt. Both paths give you a stake in the makers of the sought-after educational products of the future.

4

The Entertainment Boom

The Entertainment Trend

In recent years, Hollywood has dumped clay models and stop motion animation in favor of the computerized genius of a quiet giant: Silicon Graphics (SGI). With the acquisition of two software design companies in February 1995, SGI became the leading graphic tool design company for Hollywood. With a mastery of superb computerized special effects, like those found in Star Wars and Jurassic Park, SGI has made itself a "one-stop shop" for the movie industry. In Hollywood, any technology that facilitates bringing imagination to life is guaranteed an audience. If this is the case, technology companies that promise to bring that wonder into our homes will surely reap great rewards.

Currently, a significant transformation is occurring within the entertainment industry. The combination of new and existing technology within various media will soon unleash a vast world of information on an unsuspecting public. Computers, telephones, televisions, and optical fibers will enable anyone to join the race on the expanding *information superhighway* as long as they are willing to pay the price.

Information Superhighway

Three basic components make up the information super-highway: content, distribution, and computing. *Content* is the product, or vehicle, that travels the highway, *distribution* sends "bits" of content to the television or computer, and *computing* involves converting these bits into their intended form when they arrive at our home systems.

We've all heard about this highway, and what lies ahead for us promises to be revolutionary. Indeed, advances in technology are allowing what was once regarded as pure fantasy to be not only possible, but attainable. Anyone who owns a television will be able to participate in the exchange of information that will flood communication lines and connect households to endless outside sources. Regardless of the hype you've heard about the new wave of technology, not all the players involved in it will make money; it is possible that relatively few will. New advances in this field always promise a lot, but when ideas finally take shape, the biggest initial participants are often nowhere to be found.

It is important to keep in mind while searching for quality investments that the companies with staying power might not be visible at first, but they will grow steadily as others drop out of sight.

Success with Cellular Phone Technology

When the cellular phone business first caught the public's attention, several huge sales organizations were ready to deliver telephones. While most of them have floundered, the ones that have thrived are the businesses that provided the products themselves. For example, Motorola, who supplied telephone hardware, and McCaw, who added software technology, did very well. Each addressed a specific area of production and both companies had the capital required to develop a strong product. As a result, they possessed staying power where other, less competitive companies did not. Combined, Motorola and McCaw have been able to create somewhat of an oligopoly in the cellular phone industry because the collective product they offer is superior to that of their competitors, and because they were quick to deliver. Most other companies cannot compete with the quality and price of the phones they make nor their lines of distribution.

Entertainment Systems Adapt to New Technology

The technology involved in the cellular phone business has made it a part of the fast-paced information superhighway. At the same rate, entertainment systems that use this new technology will take shape and join in. As this happens, consumers will demand high-performance "vehicles" in order to participate in the race. In the future, there may be 500 television channels, but the public will demand interesting programs to fill them. Advances in technology will greatly affect all areas of the television industry, from manufacturing TVs to developing programming. New transmission systems will deliver information through fiber optics at an astounding rate and, with the addition of computers, usage possibilities seem endless. Anyone who owns a television will be able to use it as a communication vehicle.

Since television was developed before World War II, it has worked in the same way. Electrical waves are continuously sent either to an antenna or through a cable to the television. At that point, these waves are converted to electrons, called *analog signals,* which are sprayed onto the picture tube. The analog system functions perfectly well, but it will not integrate effectively with advanced technology. Instead, a new digital system has been developed as a part of the new package that will accept many more channels and a substantially sharper picture than the analog system. Not only will this system deliver an hour's worth of video signals in mere seconds, it will also let the viewer choose and otherwise control what is shown on the television.

In the digital system, all information comes in bits of either 1s or 0s, like the dots and dashes of the Morse code. These information bits can be manipulated to translate into precise signals. They can also be compressed to accommodate more information over the same transmission capacity, known as *bandwidth.*

In the past, a bandwidth shortage restricted television to showing only a few channels and the viewer to passively watching what was on the screen. Now, however, bandwidth capacity is becoming unlimited and is expanding rapidly because of changes in how information is conveyed. Previously, copper wire carried signals. Today, glass optical fiber is used. One strand can carry 150,000 times more information than one copper wire; millions of bits will travel through these glass fibers.

The bits may deliver vastly different media: opera or Madonna, Shakespeare or the *National Enquirer,* Leonardo da Vinci or Bart Simpson. Whether it is art, literature, or music, it will all travel over the same superhighway. Eventually, the traditional lines distinguishing among books, television, radio, newspapers, and first-run movies will unite.

Computers Carry the Message

To capitalize on the vast amount of information available, individuals will need computers that interpret the signals and translate their messages to the viewer/user. The first of these will be set-top boxes, like cable boxes, which will act as signal receptors and send information onto the television screen. Eventually, however, computers will be built into the systems, and interactive television will become a mainstay in our lives. Our televisions will become an information appliance; a vehicle for interactive media and an end station of the information highway. Fiber optic telephone wires will deliver not just voices and sound, but text and pictures as well, all to our television sets. As we connect keyboards and printers to televisions we will have the ability to access worlds of information and communicate with others from our homes.

Content Is Key

Of the three components involved in the information superhighway, content is the most important and the most likely to give future value, for without it, all the distribution and computing would be useless. The Internet system is one of the most efficient content delivery systems. It is unequivocally the most efficient and plentiful worldwide source of information. Designed by the U.S. Department of Defense, the Internet is the ultimate superhighway, and can send unobstructed signals anywhere in the world in seconds. Demand for this content provider has been overwhelming, and as a result, its usage has increased by 100 percent every year. Riders of the Internet, such as Compuserve, Time Warner Cable Interactive, and America Online, are flourishing since they can offer their users the efficiency and plethora of information available through the Internet as well as their own special services. They are the most important vehicles on the information superhighway.

America Online

America Online has become America's leading computer online service. It provides electronic mail, conferencing, computing support, software, electronic magazines and newspapers, as well as online educational classes. In January 1993, the service had approximately 600,000 subscribers in the United States. In December 1996, that number had grown to more than seven million and is expected to increase by 250,000 per month for the foreseeable future. While Compuserve is currently the largest global service, with more than three million international customers, America Online is taking steps to expand its services into Europe and Japan. Already, it has joined forces with Bertelsmann, a German media company already well established in America, to offer Europeans information and communication services through personal computers. America Online currently has more than 300,000 European subscribers and hopes to have a million subscribers outside the United States by September 1997.

Major reasons for America Online's subscription success have been its aggressive marketing, its free trial packages, its relative simplicity, and most importantly, its push toward giving its users access to the Internet. Just as there has been a rapid increase in America Online users, there has been a corresponding increase in the company's share price. Its market value has soared from $220 million in January 1993 to nearly $3.6 billion in January 1997. Earnings have increased 1,300 percent from 1994 to 1996, and it expects more than 40 percent average annual growth over the next two years. Given the stock's performance, this bet on growth has been a winner.

Much turbulence is in store for computer companies rallying for a firm position in the entertainment arena, and there will be a struggle for the top as companies try to bring online type technology to our television sets. The conflict will revolve around the design of the so-called *set-top boxes*—the mini-computers that will direct the flow of information bits into our televisions. The computer industry has been fighting small battles for the past few years over cost and distribution rights. Price wars and a generally smaller market than had been predicted have caused computer companies to scramble to thrive and even survive. These companies see the set-top box as a potential savior, and many firms are designing systems for the new fiber networks.

The biggest problem today is that none of these proposed systems will be compatible with any other and therefore will restrict the ability to communicate with other users. The same problem presents itself on the superhighway already between America Online, Compuserve, and other competing systems. None has the ability to communicate with another, so the most efficient (e.g., America Online) will slowly pull ahead of the competition as their offerings and membership increase. In the entertainment world, a situation is emerging whereby many, if not most, of these developing systems will fall by the wayside.

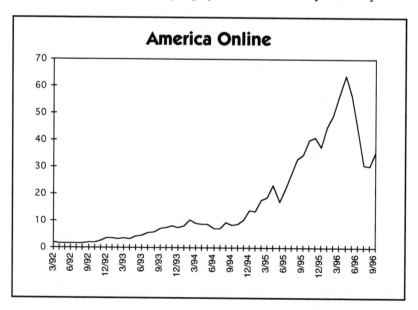

The list of companies that will be directly or indirectly fighting it out is long and the companies famous: Apple Computer, Intel, Silicon Graphics, IBM, and Sun Microsystems in the traditional computer area; Matsushita, Philips, and Sony in the consumer electronic area; and even video game giants like Sega, Nintendo, and 3DO. All these and many more less famous firms are hoping to control the set-top market.

Microsoft

Of the battling parties, Microsoft will most likely reign because of its overall dominance in the computer industry today. This position has Microsoft competitors worried; they reason that if Microsoft triumphs in this new bout of computer wars, it will be unassailable. To prevent a landslide, the competitors may join forces to thwart Microsoft's victory. If such a conglomerate were to form, it is possible that it might develop a multilink system to connect several different systems and increase compatibility, thus expanding communications.

In light of the uncertainty surrounding this computer war, investors should stay on the sidelines until the picture becomes clearer. It is entirely possible that there will be no way for an investor to choose sides and get good value. Outside of blind

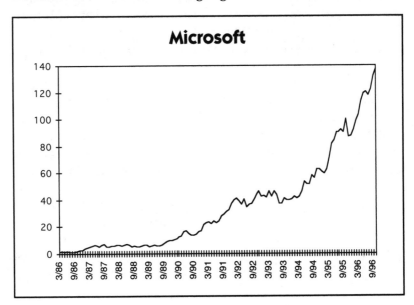

luck (if by chance the right one is chosen early enough), by the time the winner becomes clear to the general market, industry insiders will already have bid up its stock price. Thus, the big money to be made by choosing the winner of the computing wars will not often be made by individual investors, but rather it will likely be made from them. Nonetheless, Microsoft remains a company to watch. Apart from its dominance in computing, it is also working hard to establish itself as a maker of content—of vehicles. It plans to have a foot in each area, a very smart place to stand.

Viacom

When television becomes the center of our home computer systems, companies that can provide Internet-like products and quality programming will have a distinct advantage. As of now, Viacom Inc. is one of the largest single owners of content. That alone should make it interesting to an investor. Viacom's high quality programs target all age groups but generally cater to children, an incredible growth area. If you have young children and subscribe to cable television, chances are that the channel is often tuned to Viacom's Nickelodeon, which provides all-day children's entertainment. Moving up the age ladder, Viacom virtually owns the rock video market with both MTV and VH-1, which since their inception, have been the most influential television programming for preteen to college audiences. Baby boomers (and insomniacs) love "Nick at Nite," also on Nickelodeon, which brings back the classic television shows of the 1950s and 1960s. The Viacom empire also owns part of the Lifetime channel, as well as Comedy Central, and the All News Channel and is considering splitting up many of these holdings into channels that will each aim at more specific audiences (several types of music video channels, for example).

Viacom also owns Showtime and the Movie Channel. It syndicates "Roseanne" and "The Cosby Show," two of the most popular shows in television history. It also produces other successful programs, such as "Matlock" and the "Montel

Paramount and Warner Brothers are leading this consolidation trend and preparing themselves for the race to come by bringing independent broadcast stations into their network. At last count, there were only 280 independent stations left in the United States. It made more sense for Disney to buy a ready-made network, like ABC, complete with its hundreds of affiliates. As a sturdy content producer itself, as well as a major distributor, ABC was a natural buyout candidate. The same holds true for the remaining independent networks.

News Corporation

The entertainment industry is changing globally but American products remain the most popular by a landslide. In fact, the entertainment industry is always among the top three exporters in the United States. Foreign companies, like Rupert Murdoch's News Corporation, or News Corp, rely on American content for profits.

News Corp is one of the world's largest media companies and has a great track record for starting up successful major media businesses. It already owns the celebrated Fox network in the United States and Sky Television in Europe, and in the growing Asian market, News Corp's Star TV will continue on its profitable path to success. Because it is headquartered in Australia, News Corp is accessible to and has strong ties with various Asian markets.

News Corp also owns the 20th Century Fox movie studios. In the more mainstream media, it owns a string of Australian and British newspapers, TV Guide, and HarperCollins book publishers. While each of these is thought of as traditional entertainment, many have a new twist. Recently, HarperCollins announced an innovative new line of products on CD-ROM disks, such as a dictionary of sign language, that allow the user to type in any one of five languages and be shown the appropriate sign. Such niche markets will be profitable, but the big money will be in mass media, an area in which Asia offers much growth potential.

Currently, News Corp's Star TV network beams five channels to 53 countries in Asia. It concentrates in China and India

Williams Show." Finally, it produces movies for its movie channels. With its purchase of Paramount Communications Inc. and Blockbuster Entertainment in 1994, Viacom added thousands of movie titles to its huge television and video library. Now, it not only has the ability to fill several networks with classic shows, it also has the licensing and distribution rights for products (e.g., as videos) derived from these shows and the vast Blockbuster archives.

Viacom has a firm foothold in the content business and is a leader. As Chairman Sumner Redstone states in early 1994, "Viacom is at the beginning of a new dynamic cycle of growth" and the astounding revenues that year (revenues rose from $530 million to $2.7 billion in 1994) do not even reflect a year's impact of the Paramount and Blockbuster operations (1995 revenues reflecting those operations rose to $11.7 billion). The company's profits began to grow steadily in 1992, but the figures from 1994 and 1995, combined with 1996 earnings estimates of approximately $16 billion, suggest that the best is yet to come.

Up front, network operators will have a lot of power as the superhighway takes shape, as they will probably decide which type of computer will run the set-top boxes. The content companies see this as an attempt by the networks to control what the public views. As *The Economist* (February 12, 1994) points out in a summary of this industry: "Even the biggest [of the content companies], Viacom, fear[s] that network operators will use proprietary standards to limit their access to viewers; that the set-top box will be a 'tollbooth' through which they can pass only by making a deal to put their content on the network owner's server." These fears are probably exaggerated due to the fact that the distributors need content and will compete for broadcast rights of the best products. Actually, the distributor's position will be much more vulnerable than that of the content people because there will be a great deal of competition among networks and only those who provide the best quality content will really excel. Distributors' as well as computer companies' success weighs heavily on the ability and willingness of the consumer to invest in the new systems.

The network operators may wish to limit access to their programming, but chances are overwhelming that avenues will have to be open. In most places, consumers will have at least two and even three choices of how to get their information. One of their options may be the very successful DirecTV, which offers directly to viewers, through its own two satellites, up to 150 channels of digital television. Instead of using today's big satellite dishes, consumers will be able to receive all DirecTV channels with 18-inch antennas costing a fraction of the big dish price.

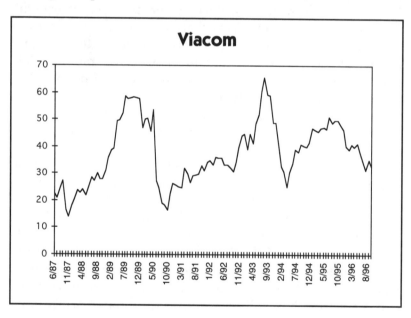

All fiber operators will have to compete with DirecTV, but, even if DirecTV acquires a geographic area in which it is the only purveyor of content, the government is likely to force them to keep the gates open to all content providers. They will have little excuse not to since the bandwidth revolution will offer hundreds of channels, and there will be room for everyone who has something interesting and entertaining to show.

Many areas will have two competing distributors in addition to DirecTV. There will be fierce competition, and the best way for them to compete will be to offer either the lowest price or the most content. The tendency will be for operators to stock up on content.

Remember that as an investor, it is wisest to choose companies with one foot in the content area and the other in the distribution area; that is, to invest in companies that create programs as well as transport them. Presently, big companies like Pacific Bell and Southwestern Bell, Comcast, and Hughes Aircraft are not positioned competitively. These telephone companies and Hughes (which owns DirecTV's satellites) are solely distributors. Competition has prompted many compa nies involved in the entertainment race to fortify themselves. Essentially, anything that has appeal on paper, on television on the silver screen, or on the radio can be used in other medi formats. A flat piece of paper can be "brought to life" throug multimedia and made interactive on the "information supe highway." Through the constant broadening, merging, ai blurring of media's distinguishing lines, companies find ea other useful in furthering their goal of entertaining you, th customer. For instance, AT&T recently purchased NCR, a m ufacturer of high-tech computers and PCs, and McCaw, wireless cellular force. In anticipation of a tough race, AT has solidified its position as a top competitor in both the tribution and computer fields. Similarly, the Viaco Paramount/Blockbuster merger has created a virtually sufficient content/distribution system. Again, companies these with two feet in the door are more likely to lead the

Investors should watch closely for distributors tha also in the content business like ABC, CBS, NBC, and Warner. Of these, CBS is the most interesting. It was the in network television's heyday during the 1950s and and ironically, it may again become a leader, this time new technology.

ABC is also an interesting story in that it was purcha the Disney Corporation in 1996. Disney is the last ren independent Hollywood studio. Time Warner owns Brothers, and Paramount has been bought by Viaco QVC. Acquiring the television network should s Disney's content distribution. Disney is a great cont ducer, but it is not likely to be bought. Indeed, with it balance sheet and need for easier distribution, Disney buy ABC, as the movie studios seek to build netv broadcasters to distribute their shows.

and though these make up the bulk of Star's Asian penetration, the growth potential there is astonishing. India is almost certainly the Asian country with the most growth potential because it is one of the world's most populous countries and has one of the fastest emerging economies. The unfortunate explosion of the Apstar-2 satellite rocket in January 1995 carried with it the intentions of many Star TV competitors, MTV for one. The Apstar-2 would have dealt a serious blow to Star because it would have broken its stranglehold over the largely English-speaking Indian market. Now, however, its participants must look for less effective alternatives. The misfortune gives Star a reprieve and more time to develop its programming, which could keep it successfully afloat in the case of another competitive onslaught. Star has established a special channel combining sports, music, and international movies for the southeast Asian market.

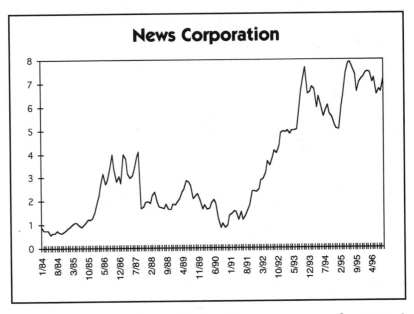

If you are familiar with the Fox network in the United States, you know that it will not win many awards for intellectual programming. Its purpose, as that of the Star network, is entertainment aimed at a mass level. Countries around the world, even those whose people don't speak English, are showing a hunger for English language-based, and especially American, entertainment, and there is nothing on the horizon that suggests a popular alternative. As long as the content and distribution are in place, there will be a growing international audience to enjoy the results.

Television Broadcasts Ltd.

Television Broadcasts Ltd. (TVB) is Hong Kong's largest television company. It operates two television stations in Hong Kong: Pearl, an English-language channel; and Jade, which broadcasts in Cantonese. TVB is also engaged in program production and other broadcasting-related activities, and it has been a leading program provider in the Chinese language for many years. Through subsidiaries, the company is involved in investment holding and animation production. In 1993, TVB launched a satellite-television service in Taiwan. The super-channel "TVBS1" is the core product contributing 95 percent of revenues and profit/losses from Taiwan; the follow-up, "TVBS2," has attracted 100,000 subscribers since its launch in September 1993. TVB currently services 100 percent of the Hong Kong audience compared to Star TV's 40 percent.

TVB's foremost market is currently Hong Kong's terrestrial broadcasting, where there are about 1.6 million television households, with a 98 percent penetration. Jade has the dominant market share for Hong Kong's prime-time Chinese viewers, garnering about 84 percent of all Chinese-language television advertising revenues in the Territory. TVB has a program library of approximately 75,000 hours, growing at 5,000 hours per year, and about 60 percent of these program hours have rebroadcasting and high hidden value in that they carry recognizable names and continuity that secure ongoing demand.

TVB's first Taiwan satellite channel, TVBS1, was launched in September 1993, broadcasting 15 hours per day. Its subscribers are the 50 cable operators of Taiwan, offering a penetration of 1.2 million households. Revenues are generated through advertising time slots and a nominal fee from the subscribers.

In late 1993, a consortium was formed including TVB, Turner Broadcasting, HBO, ESPN Asia, and Discovery Communications. The group has jointly leased nine transponders on the 1994 Apstar-1 satellite to further increase their potential television audience. "The group also shares the will to cooperate at every step, from programming to transmission, distribution, and marketing," said S.K. Fung, general manager of TVB International. This strong lineup would seem to place the TVB group ahead of its competition for the satellite television market in the region. The main competition in this area is from Rupert Murdoch's Star television satellite operation.

China's population of almost 1.2 billion consists of 288 million households, 34.7 percent of which have televisions, or 100 million television households. While the broadcasting business in Hong Kong still accounts for some 80 percent of TVB's profits, by 1999 it's expected that Taiwan and China will contribute nearly half the company's profits. Some analysts forecast total Chinese television advertising revenues could reach US$2.8 billion by 1999. Obviously, even a small percentage of total Chinese television advertising revenues would be substantial.

The 1994 launch of TVB's Apstar-1 satellite opened all areas of China to television. In 1997, it is expected that the China effort will continue to expand, with close links to be forged with government cable operators in China's major cities, where cable penetration of television households is growing at a rapid pace. The Chinese government is encouraging the development of cable systems in mainland China as the best means of controlling what is broadcast. As its long-term initiative, TVB aims to syndicate the state networks and create an international market for advertising, thus bolstering its revenues even further.

Censorship by the Chinese government has been a fear for all media companies operating in the region. TVB has shown itself to be pliant in this area, declining in the past to air programs considered critical of the Chinese government. Paradoxically, Chinese censorship could benefit TVB, because a significant part of the company's program library is nonpolitical and not Western-oriented. What few people tend to recognize is that China's tendencies fall toward more capitalistic

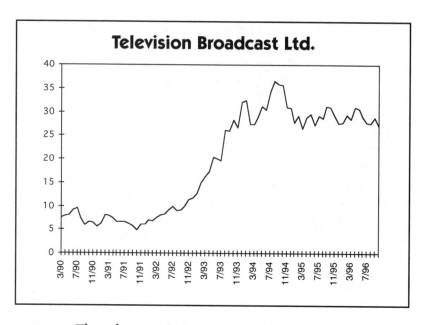

patterns. There have only been about 50 years of Communist order versus more than 2,000 years of a capitalistic, entrepreneurial society; the cultural conditioning that will allow for growth and competitive markets it already in place. That is good news for global solicitors.

Berjaya Leisure

We have looked already at the fast-growing economy of Malaysia from the perspective of its amazing ability to produce lower-cost manufactured goods. The workers are low-paid by Western standards, yet the workers themselves have experienced a surge in material prosperity over the past 20 years.

With their newfound wealth, Malaysians are looking for ways to entertain themselves with their money, and gambling is one of their favorite recreations. The numbers forecast industry is like our U.S. lotto, consisting of picking numbers in order to win prizes. In Malaysia, the legal lotto industry generates annual sales of about US$2 billion.

One Malaysian company, Berjaya Leisure, is providing a way to invest in the Malaysian lotto industry, while also providing diversified investments to capture growing leisure spending in Malaysia. Berjaya Leisure, its subsidiaries, and associated companies, operate through four divisions: property investment and development; hotel, resort, and recreation; investment holding; and gaming. Through its subsidiaries, the company is engaged in the operation of Toto betting, including four, five, and six-digit betting; property development and investment; development and operation of hotels and resorts; marketing and trading of consumer durable goods; manufacturing and distribution of personal care and household products; and the operation of cruise ships, an airline, and casinos. Through its associated companies, Berjaya Leisure is engaged in providing passenger ferry services and theme park and casino development.

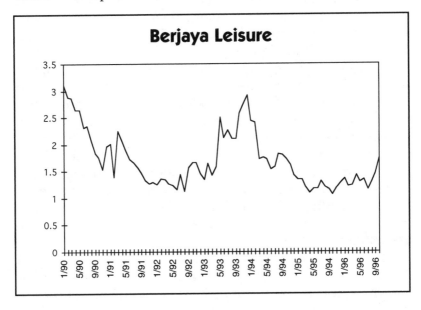

Berjaya Leisure's gaming subsidiary, Berjaya Sports Toto is probably its most valuable asset. This company has more than a 25 percent market share in the numbers forecasting market, and has no competition in the six-number "lotto" style gaming market. The company has 681 gaming outlets through the country, with 1,600 computer terminals to access the drawings. This form of recreation is available to even the poorest worker, as a minimum bet of one ringgit (less than 50 cents) allows an opportunity to win a minimum of 300,000 ringgit.

For the growing middle and upper class in Malaysia, Berjaya Leisure's other operations provide hotels and resorts, equestrian resorts, cruise ships, and casinos. Thus, Berjaya Leisure caters to all sectors of Malaysia's economically diverse population, and should benefit from this increasingly affluent and leisure-loving country.

Sony

In May 1946, Sony Corporation was founded as Tokyo Tsushin Kogyo (Tokyo Telecommunications Engineering Corporation). Since its foundation, Sony has generated many innovative products. Sony's electronics products include video and audio equipment, televisions, displays, semiconductors, electronic components, computers and computer peripherals, and telecommunications equipment. Through Sony Music Entertainment Inc. and Sony Pictures Entertainment, Sony is also strengthening its business in the worldwide music and image-based software markets. Sony is now one of the world's leaders in the consumer and industrial electronics and entertainment business areas. Sony also maintains a leading position in the development of new technologies, as evidenced by the rapid progress made in the transition from analog to digital technology in electronics and entertainment. Sony is aggressively expanding its operations outside Japan, developing and manufacturing products and providing customer services in the markets where its products are sold.

Sony Corporation of America, through its subsidiaries, is a leading manufacturer of audio and video hardware, as well as one of the world's most comprehensive entertainment companies. The company's operations include Sony Electronics Inc., which is responsible for sales, marketing, engineering and manufacturing of electronic and recording media products; Sony New Technologies, which manages new business opportunities that integrate Sony's U.S. operating companies; and Sony software companies, which include Sony Music Entertainment, Sony Pictures Entertainment Sony Retail Entertainment, which oversees Sony Theatres across the country and the development of location-based entertainment centers, Psygnosis, the videogame developer and marketer, SW Networks, a multi-media radio network providing programming through traditional broadcast and the Internet and Sony Signatures, the company's merchandise and licensing arm.

One example of an upcoming innovation in entertainment technology is the newest format in disc technology: Sony and Philips Electronics N.V. have jointly developed the MultiMedia CD, which employs a 12cm optical disc. The companies hope that this technology will generate new business opportunities in the coming multimedia age, and they have helped to develop and commercialize the digital videodisc (DVD) system, one application of the technology. The specifications of this system, which is based on a single-sided, dual-layer disc, emphasize both low-cost production and user-friendliness. Users are able to enjoy up to four and a half hours of uninterrupted playback of video images and audio signals recorded digitally on a disc the same size as a conventional CD. Offering backward compatibility with conventional CD-ROMs, the MultiMedia CD is also ideal for next-generation computer applications.

Another innovation marrying Sony's hardware expertise with its assets in entertainment content can soon be experienced on the Internet. Sony Corporation of America and Visa have joined in a multiyear agreement to offer a first-of-its-kind,

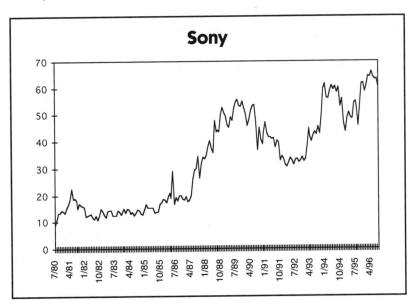

multifaceted entertainment, information and consumer transaction environment on the World Wide Web. The site, called Sony Station and launched in the fall of 1996, incorporates innovative, entertaining new programming within a "walk-through" entertainment center in cyberspace for the online consumer. As the first online entertainment center, Sony Station contains different themed "pavilions" and attractions representing programs, products, and services from the Sony Corporation of America operating companies. These companies include Sony Electronics, Sony Music Entertainment, Sony Pictures Entertainment, Sony Computer Entertainment, SW Networks, Sony Signatures (the company's licensing and merchandising operation), and Sony Retail Entertainment, including Sony Theatres.

Finally, as another example of Sony's prowess in the entertainment arena, domestic shipments of Sony Computer Entertainment Inc.'s 32-bit PlayStation videogame machine passed the 5 million mark in January 1997. Worldwide shipments of PlayStation now exceed 11 million units.

Village Roadshow

Australian-based Village Roadshow and its subsidiaries are engaged in cinemas, film distribution, film production, theme park operations, FM radio operations, and leisure center operation.

The company began as a cinema operator in Australia, and is now one of Australia's 50 largest companies, and an international entertainment conglomerate. Village Roadshow has a 40 percent market share in cinemas in Australia, building big-screen multiplexes. The company, through joint ventures, has a foothold in Asia, and plans to expand from 600 screens currently to 2,400 screens worldwide by the year 2000, by focusing on Asia and Eastern Europe. Village is committed to building powerful multiplex circuits in 14 countries: Australia, New Zealand, Singapore, Malaysia, Thailand, Taiwan, Hong Kong/China, India, Korea, Fiji, Italy, Greece, Hungary, and the Czech Republic. Village theaters in Asia and its presence in Eastern Europe puts it in areas where disposable incomes are growing dramatically.

Outside the cinema, Village Roadshow recognizes that people also want to experience entertainment at home. Thus, the company licenses and distributes home videos in Australia and Asia, while also operating an Australian recording company. Village Roadshow's radio network in Australia is the world's largest outside the United States, and is now looking to expand its radio presence in Asia.

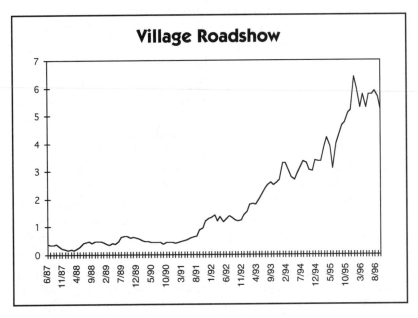

The company is also involved in the production end of the entertainment spectrum, producing television shows and theatrical movie productions. A joint venture company creates, produces, syndicates, and markets radio and television programs to approximately 35 nations.

Village Roadshow owns three major theme parks: Sea World on the Gold Coast is Australia's number one marine park. Wet'nWild Water Park is Australia's Premier water park, situated 15 minutes north of Surfers Paradise. On June 3, 1991, Village Roadshow's Warner Bros. Movie World opened in spectacular fashion and a blaze of publicity unprecedented in Australian tourism. More than six million people have visited since!

Village Roadshow is involved in a wide spectrum of entertainment activities, with management focused on opportunities in some of the fastest growing industries of the fastest growing regions around the globe. The investor should give strong consideration to this investment for the 21st century.

Hold Some "Insurance Policies"

Raymond Smith, Chairman of Bell Atlantic, captures the essence of the entertainment revolution in his thoughtful prediction: "We stand on the verge of a great flowering of intellectual property, a true Renaissance that will unleash the creative energies of inventors, entrepreneurs, hackers, artists, and dreamers."

As we enter this potentially exciting area, prudence is extremely important. Even if you firmly believe that a product, service, or industry has potential for growth, it is wise to hold investments that will not be hurt if what you expect to happen does not. For example, the likelihood that interactive television, and the information revolution in general, will revolutionize the way we are entertained is almost certain. It could be that the demand for these new services will be small and that the "tolls" on the highway to get the vehicles to our living rooms will be high. Also, building a smoothly operating highway could take years longer than planned. To prepare for such contingencies, wise investors should hold some "insurance policies." In other words, as all smart investors should know, diversity is the key to success. No matter what the odds are, look long and hard before you leap. Given sufficient information to make the proper choices, the entertainment arena will be a great place to invest over the next decade.

Investing in Both Sides of the Environmental Issue

The Environmental Trend

In recent times, our national environmental consciousness has created new opportunity and challenging obstacles within the global business community. A heightened awareness of the impact that industry can impose on nature has driven legislators to toughen their stance on pollution control and environmental protection. In doing so, they have forced certain industries to shut down, change, or adapt to new laws. Just as species evolve, migrate, and become extinct, so have certain industries. Those that modify themselves to acceptable standards and still operate efficiently will prosper with companies who clean up the mess. The others who stand to gain are foreign companies who benefit as their U. S. competitors are dismantled.

Good and Bad Effects of Government Regulation

When government meddles with industry, the result is often too many taxes and restrictions. Businesses, and even entire sectors of an economy, can be crippled or destroyed. Concerns about the environment bring to light the good and the bad effects of governmental regulation.

Lately, it has become politically fashionable to devise ways to protect the environment. As a result, we can expect the federal government to make things easy for companies that come up with good ways to clean up waste. In its zeal to attack industries that damage the environment, Washington often destroys companies or forces them to relocate. For instance, government has taken inadequate corrective actions against the industries that have dumped toxic waste into our bays and lakes, but instead has punished the fishing industry by restricting fishing or banning it altogether. From an investor's point of view, both sides of the story are worth examining.

Results of Demobilization

After spending trillions of dollars to fight the Cold War, the United States is demobilizing. Today, with that battle won and little threat of nuclear war or Communist takeover, and the government's coffers empty, justifying the need for maintaining a large military is impossible. As a result, most defense contractors are downsizing—and will continue to do so for years.

Consequently, the local economies that were sustained by military spending will dissolve. Military bases worldwide are slated to be closed. Many of these military sites have acres of contaminated land that won't be easy to clean up. Years of chemical weapons experimentation, for example, have left a trail of toxic waste throughout the world. Fortunately, each branch of the military is responsible for cleaning up its own bases. These cleanups involve the 300 to 400 bases already closed or scheduled to close under current plans, as well as bases not slated to close. About 20,000 sites are currently included in the Defense Department's Environmental Restoration Program, and more are certain to be added.

Already, the U.S. Department of Defense (DOD) is spending billions of dollars to begin what will be an extremely costly cleanup procedure. In 1993, $2 billion in contracts to private companies were given to assist in this effort. The DOD's 1991

OHM has bought companies that have expertise in all types of environmental cleanups, including asbestos eradication, hazardous waste treatment and oil spills, and recycling technologies. It is plainly trying to create a solid presence in the environmental cleanup industry. OHM can be expected to earn at least half a billion dollars per year for the foreseeable future, an exceptional record for a company whose total market capitalization is less than $200 million.

PureTec

Another company poised to take advantage of the positive side of the environmental trend is PureTec (Nasdaq, PURT), a New Jersey company that develops and sells a process for recycling large amounts of used plastic containers without harming the environment. The containers are the plastic bottles used in the soft drink industry, and the plastics used to encase bleaches, detergents, juices, and the like.

Although recycling is neither inexpensive nor highly lucrative, PureTec has turned a profit, largely because of its original and imaginative ways. One innovation is the company's reverse vending machine whereby people insert a used plastic container in a machine for recycling and collect money for it. The initial test response was so positive that PureTec had to push up production.

This approach is an example of how PureTec is ahead of competitors such as Waste Management Inc., which complains that it loses money on recycling and that it costs $150 to $200 a ton to collect from the curbside and sort household refuse. It also claims to make only $40 per ton from selling waste materials, and avoids about $30 a ton of landfill charges through recycling.

PureTec, with its patented reverse vending machine, avoids the cost of collecting and sorting. Unlike Waste Management, which tries to shift the cost of recycling to taxpayers by having towns pay for collecting plastic waste, Pure Tech patents a machine that makes it convenient for people to drop off items themselves.

PureTec is also a leading producer of medical tubing and plastic compounds for the medical device industry, precision tubing for writing instruments and spray dispensers, and lawn and garden products. The company is also a leading producer of specialty vinyl and recycled plastic materials.

PureTec seeks out niches that enable it to recycle efficiently. For example, it has patented a process that cheaply and efficiently crushes glass bottles into powder. This powder has industrial uses, particularly in the fiberglass market. To fill the hefty order of a large manufacturer of fiberglass, Schuller International, PureTec had to construct a 20,000 square foot plant in California that can turn out 400 tons of glass powder per day. California, in the forefront of recycling and environmental legislation, has mandated that every newly manufactured container sold in the state consist of a minimum amount of recycled material. The Bakersfield, California, plant is PureTec's first venture outside of the East Coast. If this plant does well, look for more expansion. PureTec has considerable room to grow over the next decade, as long as it continues its innovative approaches.

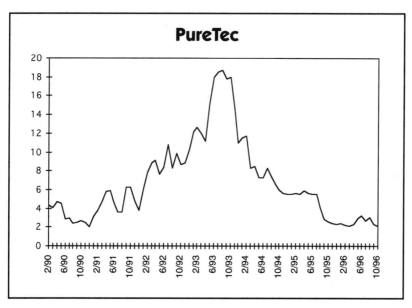

OHM and PureTec are fine examples of U.S. companies that are benefiting from the nation's zeal to clean up the environment. For every company that reaps such benefits, many others suffer. The mining industry is one that has been devastated by government restrictions. Many mines that once operated in the United States can no longer do so because of environmental litigation. Even if they escape liability for past acts, they face heavy regulations if they want to venture into new projects. In case after case, mining companies are finding that environmental concerns and low returns are preventing them from operating at a profit.

Mining activity in the United States is dwindling and increasing in countries where economic growth is deemed more important than strict environmental protection. In Asia, the mining industry has been awakened. Before it became a manufacturing giant, Asia was a continent thought to be rich in minerals. In fact, it is. Nearby Australia, which has more experience in mining, has provided a base for the expansion of mining into Asia, and the industry there is taking off.

Placer Pacific Ltd.

Australia's largest gold producer, Placer Pacific Ltd. (PLXAY), is a company that is moving steadily from its strong Australian base into Asia. Kidston, the mine Placer owns and operates in North Queensland, produces about a quarter million troy ounces a year and is large enough to be listed on the Australian Stock Exchange. Placer is also the 15th largest gold producer in the world and one of the lowest cost producers among the world's major mining companies. Because gold is the most costly among metals, it is Placer's main focus. To that end, Placer owns a part of a profitable gold mine in nearby Papua New Guinea and is exploring for gold in China, Indonesia, and the Philippines. The company is also exploring for copper throughout Australia, the Southwest Pacific, and Southeast Asia.

Over the years, Placer has established a good reputation for its dealings with the people of Asia. The company, which hires and cares for locals, is being welcomed when it seeks permission to explore and lay claims in Asian countries, with their vast regions thought to contain many minerals. With its vast interests in an increasingly profitable climate, investors should not blink at Placer.

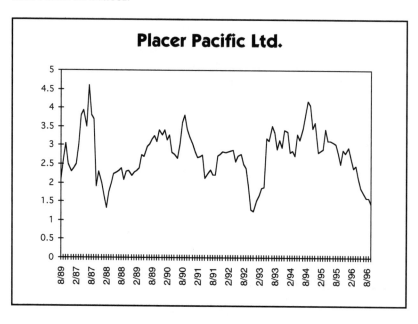

Waste Management International

Waste Management International (WMI) is a provider of waste management and related services with operations located worldwide, excluding North America. The company provides a wide range of solid and hazardous waste management services, including the collection, transportation, storage, treatment, recycling, and disposal of waste. It operates a waste-to-energy facility, develops and operates water and wastewater treatment facilities, and it performs certain related environmental services. The company currently has operations in 21 countries. In 1993, the company completed 48 acquisitions in the United Kingdom, France, Netherlands, Germany, Denmark, Italy, Sweden, Austria, Australia, New Zealand, and Taiwan.

The company also conducts research and development activities, such as using special pumps to remove leached pollutants from old landfills, and the development of filtering technology to convert oily sludge into reusable oil, clean water, and solids.

Europe, WMI's mainstay, is increasingly focusing on environmental standards. For example, a directive passed by the European Union (EU) will require the provision of primary and secondary treatment of wastewaters from households and industry. The directive also imposes strict controls and reporting requirements on the discharges of wastewaters, prohibiting the dumping of sewage, thus increasing further the volumes of sludges that will require specialized treatment and disposal, which WMI provides. The EU has shown a great willingness to impose upon its member countries European-wide environmental legislation, in response to heightened public and political concern.

Outside of Europe, particularly in emerging markets, continuing industrialization, population expansion, and urbanization have caused increased levels of pollution. The desire to sustain economic growth and address historical pollution problems in now accelerating investments in environmental infrastructure, particularly in Southeast Asia. In Thailand, for example, where WMI has a joint venture, the government has introduced a comprehensive Environmental Protection Act and is in the process of substantially upgrading and revising other existing environmental statutes. Indonesia and Malaysia are also in the process of updating or extending their legislative frameworks for the management of wastes.

In general, the company benefits substantially from the regulation of waste management and environmental services because of the effect on regulation on demand for more technologically advanced and capital intensive solutions provided by experienced companies such as WMI.

The Investor's Best Approach

It is a safe bet that demand for environmental protection will grow in the United States. This will probably be true even if average living standards fall, due to a continued shift of the manufacturing (and mining) industries elsewhere. The pro-environmental lobby is strong, and most Americans will be convinced that strict regulations against pollution will benefit everyone.

In light of this, the best approach to the environmental dilemma is twofold. First, look for companies in the United States that are innovative and clean up or recycle cheaply and efficiently. Next, look abroad for companies that pick up the slack when U.S. industries are adversely affected by environmentalism and wither away.

6

Investing in Companies That Tackle Crime

The Personal Security Trend

Every television station across America broadcasted the latest developments in the O.J. Simpson trial. Every news hour highlights another violent crime committed in someone's backyard. A five-year-old kindergarten student brings a gun to school. Pulp Fiction was one of the most popular movies of the decade. The United States spends $22 billion to comfortably house its one million plus inmates every year. Every five seconds a car theft takes place. Young gang members practice genocide in the inner cities. A woman is raped or severely beaten every 20 seconds. Billions of dollars worth of illegal drugs cross into our country every day and wind up in the hands of our children.

Crime Affects Everyone

There is no need for a market analysis or an academic study to recognize the greatest intrusion and obstacle paralyzing American society; common sense screams to us that it is crime. As today's startling statistics point out, crime affects everyone. In the past 30 years, the U.S. crime rate has increased by 300 percent, and the magnitude of these crimes is shocking. The rise of urban and suburban gangs has brought with it an alarming number of heinous crimes committed by juveniles. Even though the offenders are younger, they feel no remorse about raping, murdering, torturing, or destroying while our society sits by and allows these things to occur. And as the moral decay of America continues, so does crime and so does the need to protect ourselves from being victimized.

Personal Security an Issue

Personal insecurity is a growing trend that is taking a big toll on the productive life of our nation. Crime and fear of crime often dictate the choices people are making to leave urban areas or to commute to work, for example. Now more than ever, people willingly drive long distances to their jobs because they think the suburbs offer more security for themselves and their families than their city-workplace neighborhoods. To protect their families, parents spend their hard-earned money to send their children to private schools where, unlike more and more public schools, crime is virtually absent and children feel safe. Crime—real or imagined—has become a fact of life for many Americans.

When *Money* magazine prepared its annual "Best Places to Live in America" issue for 1996, as usual it asked its readers to identify their most important consideration in choosing a place to live. From the late 1980s to the early 1990s, clean water was their priority. In 1996, however, a low crime rate was a primary concern of *Money* readers. Although a clean environment still gets strong consideration, Americans are beginning to fear for their safety more than they fear for their health. Whether they must relocate or arm their houses and themselves, these people refuse to let their lives be directed by crime. After considering the money and time that could be spent much more productively, the crippling economic cost of avoiding and fighting crime in the United States becomes apparent.

Companies That Provide Security

As more people are willing to spend money for protection, the companies that service their needs will profit. Among them are companies that manufacture and distribute products, such as alarm systems, locks, outdoor motion sensors, and "The Club." More and more companies continue to jump at opportunities on the "crime trend" bandwagon in an attempt to provide the security an increasingly insecure world craves. The companies spotlighted here are currently worth watching, but better investments may soon be on the scene: those with a less expensive stock value and a more desirable or effective method for combating crime.

Several U. S. companies' primary focus is battling "low-tech" crimes. For instance, Diebold, Inc. is a premier maker of locks and safes. The growth implication of this industry is obvious based on the impact of the current crime wave. Pinkerton Security and Investigation, which trains and provides security guards and investigators, is another company that stands to profit. Brink's Home Security, famous for its armored cars, also provides home security systems.

Providing security in the face of increasing crime is nearly certain to be a growth industry. A big problem for investors, however, is that it is not easy to find a blue chip "security stock" as a pure play. Brink's, for example, is operated by the Pittston Company, which participates in many fields other than the crime-security scene. As an investor, you must buy into Pittston in order to have an interest in Brink's. Likewise, the other old-line, well-known companies have been accused of no longer being competitive on the cutting edge of crime-fighting technology. Time will tell how these cornerstone players choose to fight; most likely they will be aggressive.

Corrections Corporation of America

One U.S. company that is becoming better known in a different light is the Corrections Corporation of America, a builder of prisons. CCA, a pure play, claims to be far more efficient and cost-effective in its construction than the government contractors who currently monopolize the prison building industry. Traditional government builders take from two to five years to get a new prison up and running, while Corrections Corporation needs just a year. Although it claims to run prisons much more cheaply than state correction facilities do, this company has not yet been allowed to prove itself. It is no surprise that state-run prison operators, fearing perhaps that they will lose their jobs, have publicized enough negative allegations about would-be private competitors to make things hard for them. Again, time will tell. Perhaps, once budget reforms take effect, CCA's prices will be too cheap to ignore.

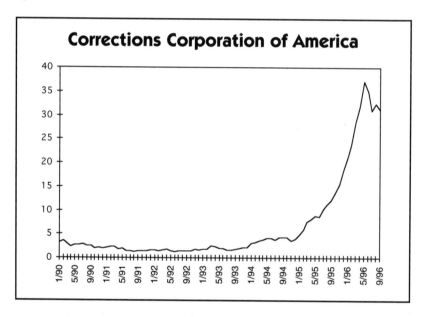

Societe Generale de Surveillance Holding

Unfortunately, the rest of the world is also not immune to crime. As a result, some of the most interesting crime-fighting technologies and companies are found beyond America's borders. Societe Generale de Surveillance Holding, based in Geneva, Switzerland, is the world's largest provider of international inspection, testing, and verification for the import/export business. It offers its clients (usually governments and large corporations) tailor-made programs in many different areas where fraud, their toughest opponent, can hold sway.

Much fraud occurs during the import and export of goods and Surveillance provides the verification techniques that help customs agents to unveil this and other types of scandals. It has also been adept at seeking out and exploiting certain niches such as offering loss-adjusting services for insurance companies, which are often the victims of dishonest scams.

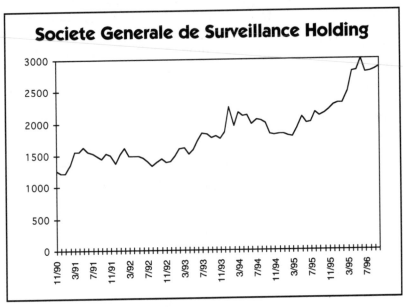

Today, uncovering fraud has become a priority in most industries, which is why Surveillance is active in so many fields. It has divisions that focus on the trade and shipping of raw materials (such as petroleum and petrochemical products), industrial and consumer goods, agriculture, and health and environmental services. Surveillance, with more than 30,000 employees, currently operates in 140 countries with 274 subsidiaries, 1,150 offices, and 291 laboratories, and it is constantly expanding its clientele. Within only a few months last fall, for example, it signed new contracts with the governments of Indonesia, Ethiopia, and the Congo. The company's stock trades on the Zurich stock exchange and has no plans to list on U.S. exchanges.

Applied International Holdings

Another investment opportunity abroad comes from Hong Kong. Applied International Holdings is a company that manufactures home and car alarm systems and other electronic personal security devices. It also makes nonelectronic security products, such as door braces (which are also used to secure windows) and a flame-retardant treatment for home fabrics. New projects being developed include voice-activated telephones and an electronic location device for cars and other moving objects. Applied International manufactures its products very cost-effectively in China. Applied International is a new company without much of a track record, but the combination of low-cost manufacturing of high-technology security equipment with the increasing demand for such equipment sounds very promising. Applied International trades on the Hong Kong stock exchange.

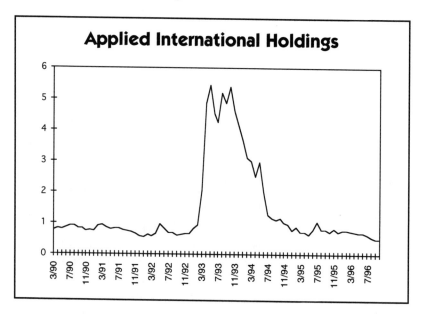

ADT

North America's largest provider of electronic security systems is ADT, a company based in Boca Raton, Florida. Because ADT trades on the New York Stock Exchange, it is easier for U.S. investors to buy than the two foreign stocks mentioned above. Like some of the "low-tech" companies mentioned earlier, ADT is not a pure play on the insecurity trend. A separate division of the company is also North America's second largest provider of automotive vehicle auction services. Financially, that aspect of the company is very stable and does not detract from its protective services, which make up the lion's share of ADT's business. Electronic security systems provided nearly $1 billion in sales in 1993, compared to $350 million in auction services, so although ADT may not be a pure play on rising crime, it comes close.

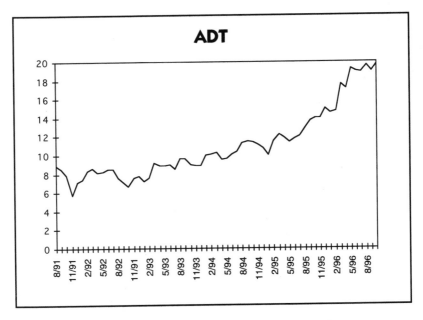

ADT is also internationalizing its products. It has been particularly successful in Great Britain, where it is the second largest provider of security systems, and it is also expanding its services to Australia. In 1996, ADT's residential customer base reached 1.1 million of which approximately 85 percent is located in the United States. As the fear of crime grows, so will this number. The number of other firms providing protection will also continue to grow and as an active investor, it is wise to keep your eyes peeled for the newcomers.

7

Investing in Biotechnology

The Biotechnology Trend

One of the most critical dilemmas greeting our world on the verge of the 21st century is the question of how to feed and care for our people. With exponential growth patterns continuing, the total population on earth is expected to double well within the next 100 years, and most of the growth will occur in the poorest nations. In anticipation of this problem, the world's food suppliers are challenged to find a way to increase current levels of food production in order to sustain the population, and pharmaceutical companies must prepare to help combat new diseases by developing affordable yet effective drugs. Fortunately, two technological sectors have been actively pursuing a solution to this crisis: the biotechnology and the agri-biotechnology sectors. Because of their scientists' efforts, one of the most exciting trends shaping up to transform life in this decade is happening in these industries.

Improved Foods and Drugs

The new technology that will give us better food and drugs is that which will allow us to rearrange the chemical makeup of plant and animal life. The idea of genetic engineering, a process that conjures up images of freakish experimentation and Frankensteins, actually has roots stretching back decades, but many practical uses for it are just now being developed. In fact, much of the food we eat today is the result of similar experimentation that introduced isolated living organisms, such as yeasts of molds, into other foods. Bread, yogurt, wine, buttermilk, cheese, and pickles all depend on this process.

Genes exist in every living thing, including plants, fruits, and vegetables, and the idea of "breeding" foods is not new at all; farmers have been tinkering with plant genes for thousands of years in an attempt to grow healthier crops or to get higher-yielding acreage. Judging by the results, Mother Nature herself is the most effective genetic engineer. Species of plants and animals have adapted and changed as long as they have existed in order to better compete in their environment.

Better Crops Through Agri-Biotechnology

Agri-biotechnology "assists" plants in the adaptation process by rendering them resistant to disease, rot, and other environmental obstacles, thus creating better crops. A process that is now on the cutting-edge of genetic engineering is the use of amazingly advanced technology to insert as little as a single gene into one plant to provide a desired change in an entire crop. This can be a gene that has been engineered either to arrest bad characteristics (like spoilage) or to engender good ones (like flavor). Scientists today have successfully altered the chemical makeup of many plants to create superior produce. Eventually, they hope to introduce the same technology to areas around the globe in order to combat the future hunger problem.

One type of produce industry that has been positively affected by genetic research and engineering, both in cost and quality, is the tomato industry. While Americans buy more tomatoes per capita than almost any other produce, they are increasingly disappointed by their flavor. In a 1993 study by the U.S. Department of Agriculture, consumers rated the tomato last on a list of 31 produce items in terms of taste satisfaction. Although the tomato market generates more than $4 billion annually in the United States, most people think the tomatoes they buy do not taste very good. Loyal consumers suffer through months of mealy, bland tomatoes every year with lingering memories of the mouth-watering succulence of the summer's sweet crop. If scientists could reproduce the August tomato year around, markets would not be able to keep them on the shelves!

Calgene

Among the companies racing to create a superior tomato is Calgene, a small Davis, California biotech company that stands among the front runners in agri-biotechnology. The company got worldwide attention in 1994 when the U.S. Food and Drug Administration (FDA) approved its genetically engineered tomato, the "Flavr Savr," which has twice the shelf life of regular vine-ripened tomatoes and needs no refrigeration. Through Campbell Soup Company-funded research and its own patented Antisense technology, Calgene scientists isolated and copied the gene that "tells" a tomato to get soft, causing it to lose flavor. They then reinserted the gene backwards, which, in its altered state, told the tomato not to get soft. As a result, Calgene marketed the first genetically engineered tomato.

Since its approval in May 1994, the Flavr Savr tomatoes have been sold in more than 3,000 stores. Hoping to duplicate that performance, Calgene continues to develop more products, such as herbicide-resistant cotton and low-fat canola oils, which, upon their success, will further boost Calgene's revenues. The acceptance of the "Flavr Savr" also prompted Calgene to redirect spending by cutting back on its expensive research staff and focusing more on the profitable production of the new tomatoes, which has enabled it to maintain a cash balance. Also, in December 1996, the company was granted a third patent involving high-level foreign gene expression in plant plastids. Plastid transformation technology could be applied to the production of raw materials for pharmaceutical products, "biodegradable" plastics, specific high-level expression of insect and herbicide resistant traits in plants and modification of plant starches and seed oils. With the stock price hovering near its 12-month low ($4 1/4 as of July 24, 1996), Calgene is very appealing. Shareholders are hoping for the price to climb back to its May 1994 position of $15 and it looks as though it may be headed in that direction.

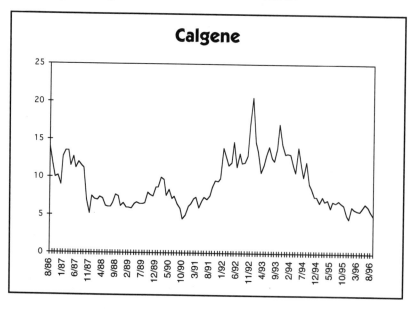

Novo Nordisk

Unlike Calgene and DNAP, which are fairly young, small U.S. companies, Novo Nordisk is an old, established European blue chip. But like them, it is very much up to date in the agri-bio area. While it is much higher priced than either Calgene or DNAP, Novo carries with it much less risk and therefore provides an anchor in the turbulent seas of agri-biotech.

If you've heard of Novo, it may have been in connection with insulin, the hormone found in animal pancreas. Novo has been producing insulin since 1925, just after it was discovered and linked to the treatment of diabetes, and currently provides about a third of the world's supply. Novo Industries was born in the basement laboratories of two Danish doctors, the Pederson brothers, who began producing "Insulin Novo" based on a tip from a Danish Nobel scientist privy to the first insulin discovery in Toronto.

Since its inception, research and development has remained a priority for Novo, much of it involving the sort of animal and plant testing that has resulted in longer and better lives for millions of people. For instance, if you were wounded in World War II, or indeed anytime from 1938 to 1950, the wound was most likely sutured with a surgical thread called *catgut*. Novo developed this material by sterilizing and autoclaving sheep guts. During World War II, Novo also began to extract enzymes from animal glands that were ultimately used by industry to better manufacture countless goods. Today, Novo is by far the largest producer of industrial enzymes, producing half of the world's supply.

A crowning success came with Novo's production of penicillin. When it became clear to scientists that penicillin was a form of bacteria, Novo's employees examined virtually everything from old ski boots to jars of jelly in hot pursuit of the wonder drug. Upon its discovery, Novo became one of the first commercial producers of penicillin. Today, Novo is not only a major player in that market, but it has also expanded its role and now produces so-called second generation antibiotics. These substances are effective in patients allergic to penicillin and fight harmful bacteria resistant to it. Novo also holds the patent for heparin, an organic substance that fights blood clots.

Not all of Novo's products involve using animal organs. In fact, many of its more recent successes involve producing industrial enzymes by means of fermentation of plant microorganisms. These have been used in the manufacture of products ranging from detergents to textiles. In effect, Novo products may not only have made your shirt, they may help to clean it, too.

Insulin, which the company is constantly improving, remains Novo's mainstay and continues to demand its attention. For example, during the 1980s, Novo finally developed a process by which porcine insulin could be changed into an exact copy of that found in the human body. As an indirect result of this discovery, Novo established a genetic laboratory to manufacture both new enzymes and hormones. The potential applications for this are vast, ranging from pollution control to fuel alcohol for engines to new sources of food protein.

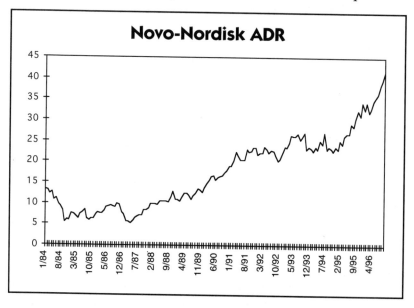

Novo is a Danish company and is thus fortified in Danish krone, though its stock trades in New York (in ADR form) and London as well as in Copenhagen. The Danish currency has been among the world's strongest and is fortified through ties to the German mark. The krone, like all major European currencies, has been rising against the dollar since about 1970. As a result, the price of Novo stock in dollar terms has risen 500 percent in the past ten years. Thus, owning the stock has been a good way for Americans to protect themselves against a fall in the dollar's value, just like owning a stock denominated in any stronger currency would be. If you plan to diversify your portfolio into the exciting area of agri-biotechnology, your holdings should include Novo. The stock won't likely rise in percentage terms as much as that of Calgene or DNAP if these two reach their potential, but Novo has pioneered "tomorrow's advances" for nearly 70 years and shows no sign of letting up.

Microcide Pharmaceuticals

Microcide Pharmaceuticals, a biopharmaceutical company, was founded in 1992 to discover, develop, and commercialize novel antibiotics for the treatment of serious bacterial infections. The company's programs address the growing problem of bacterial drug resistance through two principal themes: Targeted Antibiotics, which develops novel antibiotics, and Targeted Genomics, which utilizes bacterial genetics to discover new classes of antibiotics and new treatments for bacterial disease.

Bacteria have great survival capacity, mutating either from their own genetic diversity or borrowing the genetic structures of related bacteria, to resist medical antibiotics. For example, penicillin-resistant strains of bacteria developed soon after penicillin's introduction in the 1940s. In recent times, doctors have tended to overprescribe antibiotics, leading to increasing numbers of antibiotic-resistant strains. In particular, it is feared that virulent staph infections could become untreatable in the future.

The antibiotics market is the third largest pharmaceutical market, with global sales of $22.9 billion in 1995. This market is increasingly important, as there is a growing crisis within the medical community caused by antibiotic-resistant bacteria. In the U.S. alone, these bacteria result in eight million days of extended hospital stay, accounting for more than $4 billion in additional health care costs annually. The specific problematic bacteria that Microcide addresses in its research are responsible for 44 percent of the approximately two million hospital-acquired infections occurring annually in the United States.

It appears that the pharmaceutical industry has put too much faith in medicinal chemistry solutions, spending too little effort on understanding the molecular biology of resistant bacteria. The founder of Microcide foresaw the looming problem of resistance, and created a company of 80 people, three corporate partners, and $50 million cash in preparation for launching a stream of novel antibiotic cures by the year 2001.

In Microcide's Essential Genes Program, the company has identified approximately 80 essential gene targets that are being incorporated into a screening system to discover new classes of antibiotics. In another program, the company is developing and utilizing new molecular genetics technologies to discover and develop new therapeutic agents.

Microcide has entered into collaborative agreements with three major pharmaceutical companies to enhance specific discovery and development programs. Microcide is collaborating with Ortho Pharmaceuticals, a Johnson & Johnson company to discover new classes of antibiotics and bacteria inhibitors. Microcide is collaborating with Daiichi Pharmaceuticals to develop another class of bacterial inhibitors. Additionally, Microcide is collaborating with Pfizer to implement its essential gene and multichannel screening system to discover novel classes of antibiotics.

Microcide was first offered to the public in 1996 and is presently still in its product-development phase, with profitability hoped for in the 21st century. An investment today could potentially provide a ground floor opportunity in the bio-pharmaceutical trend of tomorrow.

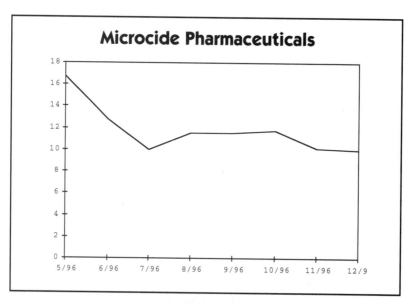

Everyone Will Benefit

The most exciting news about agri-biotechnology is that everyone will benefit from it. The advances taking shape promise to revolutionize the agricultural industry tremendously by increasing productivity, yielding healthier, high-percentage crops, and by increasing the durability of the produce itself while keeping prices reasonable. We are now in the cradle of development, and the final goal is to produce plentiful crops that are naturally resistant to disease and bugs and to do away with the need for chemicals that are harmful to the environment. In the same light, companies like Novo that continue to develop organic medicines and textiles will also contribute to the improvement of our environment and livelihood. Some other companies to watch are ADM, Pioneer Hybrid, DuPont, and Dow Chemical, all of which participate generously in the areas of biotech research and development. The biotechnology industry is fascinating, and it is a safe bet that advances and more new companies will spring up fast. It will pay to keep an eye on developments here.

Chapter

8

Investing in the Telecommunications Boom

The Telecommunications Trend

Two stories capture what this chapter is about. Both were told by Paul Theroux, the famous travel writer, in a 1993 *Harper's Magazine* story, after he returned from China's most bustling provinces.

While in China, Theroux visited a factory where gold-plated jewelry was being made. As he watched a golden mushroom being polished, the factory manager, a Welshman, told him, "A polisher can do only five an hour. That's why you cannot afford to polish in Europe." An Irish worker earns about $25 an hour for this skill—and Ireland has one of the lowest wage rates in Europe. The Chinese polisher was doing the same job just as well for 50 cents an hour.

Consider that. The Chinese will work for 2 percent of the European's wage. In other words, 50 times the production per dollar spent comes from the Chinese craftsmen. If you wanted to manufacture a product, where would you go? This simple example, says Theroux so rightly, shows the reason that the world's manufacturing base has moved to the East.

Theroux tells another story, this one about Zhuhai, a city on the border of the Portuguese colony of Macau. Only a few years earlier it had been a sleepy village. Now, says Theroux, "In every restaurant and lobby bar there [are] Chinese talking on cellular phones; and on one occasion at each of the six tables around me there was someone talking on a phone. Five years ago it was almost impossible to make a call from the best hotel. The boom in telecommunications is part of the Chinese miracle, and even prostitutes wear beepers."

Shenzhen, like Zhuhai, is a border town, and it is also booming. But both these border towns represent only a tiny fraction of 1 percent of the Chinese land and population. Think of how many telephones can be used in the hinterland.

China makes almost all the telephones the Chinese use—and many more for export. As in the jewelry business example, the Chinese work seven days a week (with occasional days off) from morning until late at night to make telephones for Taiwanese companies at wages of about $35 a month.

But there is far more to a telecommunications system than just telephones. Cables, wiring, and switching stations are also needed. And though much of the labor may be supplied by the Chinese, the capital and expertise will come from foreign companies that have had the foresight to become involved in these booming Chinese provinces. Ultimately, the profits from such investments will go to them.

Telecommunications Growth in Other Parts of the World

The telecommunications boom happening in some areas of China is also happening in other parts of the world. People in most developed countries, however, have long gotten used to having all the telephones they want. For example, in the United States, there are 55 lines for every 100 Americans; in Switzerland, there are 65 lines per 100 people; and in Sweden, there are 70. But many countries have amazingly few telephone lines per person. The Philippines, with a population of 63 million, has a paltry 1.3 lines per 100 people. India and China have between them more than one-third the world's population but each has less than one telephone line per 100 inhabitants.

Clearly, the room for growth in this industry is enormous. This is especially true for China, with its vibrant economy, where that growth will be explosive. The Beijing government wants to quadruple the number of telephone lines by 2000. This would make 80 million lines where only 20 million now exist. This 60-million line increase is equal to three times the entire existing telephone network in Great Britain. But even with this projected growth, and even if its population grows little during the next six years, China will still enter the 21st century with barely four lines per 100 people. Already Britain has 44 lines, more than ten times the projected Chinese rate.

This is not the situation in Hong Kong, however. Just over the border from China, there are already 49 lines per 100 people. This is more than Britain's ratio and shows what is possible in China when it takes over Hong Kong in 1997. If China increases its telephone line ratio to match the ratio that Hong Kong has now, it would mean a staggering increase of 600 million telephone lines.

China is currently relying on Hong Kong Telecom to help the most booming regions of China—the areas closest to Hong Kong—vault into the telecommunications age. China indirectly owns 17.5 percent of the company, but Hong Kong Telecom is in an enviable position even without the "Chinese connection." It had an exclusive monopoly to provide local phone service in Hong Kong until mid-1995 and has it for long distance between Hong Kong and the rest of the world until September 30, 2006.

Cable & Wireless

Hong Kong Telecom is partly owned by one of the most exciting companies of the past century. Cable and Wireless (CWP) has been in the telecommunication business since 1872, and everywhere the British Empire expanded, so did CWP. It now operates telecom services in 50 countries; in many of them, it is the main provider. Besides its "Hong Kong connection," CWP has a direct foothold in China through its ownership of 49 percent of Hyaying Nanhai Oil Telecommunication Service.

In addition to China, the Philippines and especially Malaysia are ardently expanding their telecommunication services. Also, CWP is the leading contender to take over the state telephone monopoly in cellular phones in Taiwan. It owns 17 percent of Japan's second largest international phone company.

CWP is also a major telecom player outside of Asia. In its home market in the United Kingdom, it is a major cellular phone provider. It is also the fourth largest long distance carrier in the United States (after AT&T, MCI, and Sprint).

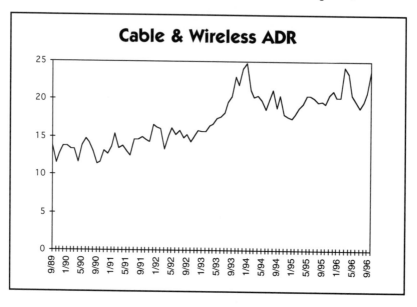

Cable & Wireless ADR

Telebras

Latin America is another area quickly moving into the first ranks of the modern world. Latin America's version of China—its largest, most populous, and potentially richest country—is Brazil. In Brazil, Telebras has the monopoly on all phone calls made in the country.

Only 6.7 percent of Brazil's 160 million people have telephone lines. This is about half the percentage of Brazil's neighbors, Argentina and Chile, and also less than Mexico's percentage. But Brazil has a larger economy than the rest of South America combined. In fact, it is one of the world's ten largest economies in terms of production.

Telebras is 57 percent owned by the Brazilian government; investors can buy only 43 percent of it. Some rumors indicate that it will become privately held, but for now it is one of the world's cheapest telecom companies. Based on current earnings, it is even cheaper; with the stock at only nine times earnings.

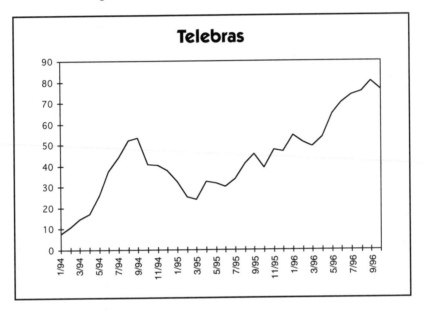

STET

About 20 years ago, Italy's economy wasn't working well and its infrastructure was sometimes primitive. This is no longer so. In fact, not since the Renaissance has Italian industry so proudly spread its wings around the world. If Northern Italy (Rome and above) and Southern Italy were separated, the North could imaginably have the world's highest standard of living, but much remains to be done. The country's telephone system, while much improved, has room to grow. All the new wealth in the North has created a huge demand for phone lines, fax lines, and cellular phones. The South, on the other hand, resembles an emerging economy, with a primitive phone company that needs to be modernized.

STET (Societa Finanziaria Telefonica SpA) is the financial holding company of the telecommunications division of IRI, the formerly state-owned industrial holding company for Italy.

STET operates through approximately 83 subsidiaries and 16 associate companies. Its principal subsidiary is the newly formed Telecom Italia, created in July 1994 from the former companies SIP, Italcable, Telespazio, IRITEL, and SIRM.

The Italian telecommunications industry has been run under state ownership through a complex structure of holding and operating companies. IRI, the state-owned industrial holding company, owns 52 percent of STET, the holding company specifically responsible for telecommunications. STET, in turn, typically holds a majority of the shares of companies responsible for network services, manufacturing, and a range of related activities. Licensing and regulation of telecoms are currently the responsibility of the Ministry of Post and Telecommunication. A changed political and economic environment has brought about a reform program, creating a single integrated network services company, Telecom Italia. As soon as practicable (expected to be late 1994 to 1995), IRI will seek to reduce, and ultimately eliminate, its shareholding in STET, thus privatizing the telecommunications industry. This would leave STET as the ultimate umbrella holding company for almost every sector of the Italian telecommunications industry—from networks, manufacturing, wireless, and satellite services to telephone directory and Yellow Pages publishing.

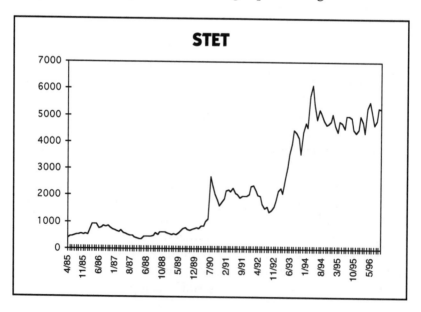

Telecom Italia

STET holds 61.5 percent of Telecom Italia, the newly unified Italian telephone network operator. Upon its formation, it immediately became the world's sixth largest telecommunications operator. It was created by uniting five companies: SIP (operating the domestic Italian telecommunications network as well as the cellular telephone network); Italcable (operating the international call traffic from Italy to countries outside Europe and some North African countries); Telespazio (operating worldwide satellite services connected to and from Italy and also providing satellite-based closed-user systems); SIRM (operating wireless marine communications services in Italy); and Iritel (operating the concession for international services linking Italy with Europe and North Africa).

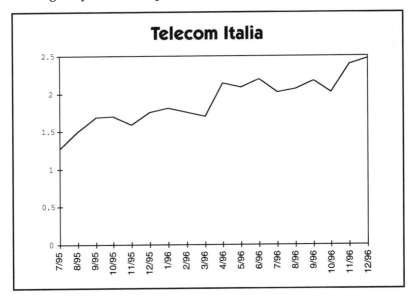

The unification of services under Telecom Italia should bring several benefits: an increase in the quality of revenues brought about by an increased focus on customer satisfaction; lower operating costs brought about by a reduction of overhead and the elimination of redundant staffing; and a coordinated capital investment plan. Additionally, while restructuring will bring economic rationalization, line growth and usage increases should continue to be above the European average.

Italy is expected to implement a tariff rate increase system based on CPI % – X % per annum, allowing telephone rates to be increased annually at the rate of inflation less a certain percentage, rather than being subjectively decided by bureaucratic fiat. This would allow the benefits of restructuring to flow through to higher profit margins and absolute profit levels, while allowing for improved planning and forecasting capabilities on the part of management.

STET is likely to continue to play a key role in the management of the telephone companies, particularly in budget and capital expenditure planning. STET will also be determining policy for overseas expansion through its control of STET International (one example of which is its involvement in Telecom Argentina, with attributable ownership of approximately 20 percent). STET's success in telecommunications equipment manufacturing should be cemented by the planned creation of a joint venture merging Italtel with the Italian manufacturing operations of German engineering conglomerate Siemens AG.

P.T. Indosat

P.T. Indonesian Satellite Corporation "Indosat" is the primary provider of international telecommunications services in Indonesia, directly linking Indonesia to approximately 215 countries and destinations worldwide. The company's primary business is to provide international switched telecom services and had a 91.7 percent share of Indonesia's total international call minutes through the third quarter 1996. Additionally, Indosat has a 35 percent stake in a GSM mobile phone operator "Telkomcel." Other services include telex, telegram, packet switched networks, and facsimile services. The company owns and operates four international gateways that route transmissions through satellite, submarine cable, and microwave networks.

Indosat was established in 1967 as a wholly owned subsidiary of ITT. In 1980, Indosat was sold in its entirety to the Indonesian Government, which in October 1994 sold 32 percent of its ownership in a global public offering. The Indonesian Government currently owns 65 percent of the company, effectively retaining control over the company's governance.

From its inception, Indosat has managed the introduction of new telecommunications technology and greatly expanded the scope of its services in Indonesia. The business of the company has grown rapidly in recent years, reflecting excellent economic growth combined with increased emphasis placed by the Indonesian government on improving the national telecommunications network. Total volume of international telecom traffic has risen from 188 million paid minutes in 1990 to 583 million paid minutes in 1996.

Indonesia has a population of 196 million, making it the world's fourth most populous nation. It is a developing nation, with a low GNP per capita of approximately $987, but real economic growth is high, averaging from 6 to 7 percent over the past ten years. There are approximately 3.3 million telephone lines in service throughout the country at present, but the government's current five-year development plan targets a tripling of phone line penetration, bringing the total to 10 million lines by 2000, and 14 million by 2,004. Current access line penetration is only 1.7 per 100 population (4.5 in the major cities), versus 60 per 100 in the United States. By the year 2000, lines per 100 population is expected to be about 4.

The Ministry of Tourism, Posts, and Telecommunications (MTPT) acts as the regulator of telecommunications services. The MTPT sets tariff policy for Indosat, and this policy is cost-oriented, formulated to promote affordability and avoid any negative impact on Indosat. Indosat's tariffs have not been materially changed since 1986, except for the introduction of discounts on evenings and weekends. The company's average rate per minute is approximately 1,950 rupiah per minute (US$0.85/min.) In the provision of international interconnections, Indosat has only one competitor, Satelindo, and this duopoly will remain until at least 2005. Currently, Indosat has more than 92 percent market share, expected to fall to about 75 percent by 2000. Indosat's competitor Satelindo is not allowed to compete with Indosat on the basis of price, meaning that competition should not put pressure on margins. Overall, the loss of market share should be more than compensated for by strong volume growth of the total market.

Indosat's strategy is to remain the market leader in Indonesian international telecommunications services.

Additionally, Indosat has taken a stake in a 30%-owned consortium to install and jointly operate additional fixed-line domestic service, a strategy the Indonesian government is pursuing to increase the rate of phone line coverage. Additionally, Indosat owns 35 percent of Telkomcel, a national GSM digital mobile phone system, one of three in Indonesia. The company has 60,000 subscribers at last report, and is expected to grow at a rapid pace. Both fixed-line and wireless investments should bring new customers to its international network.

The company's stated strategy is known as *1 + 3*, meaning expanding its core international telecommunications business, while adding three supporting businesses. The primary focus is to retain Indosat's position as the primary international telecom services provider in Indonesia. Secondarily, additional businesses are being developed, such as fixed-line operations, GSM cellular business, and now new multimedia, Internet, and broadcasting businesses being developed.

The earnings trend should remain firmly up for the foreseeable future, as Indosat's most significant variable, international connect time, is expected to increase by more than 20 percent annually through the decade. Company earnings should increase more modestly, within a range of 10 to 15 percent annually, reflecting a modest decline in market share, combined with new project costs.

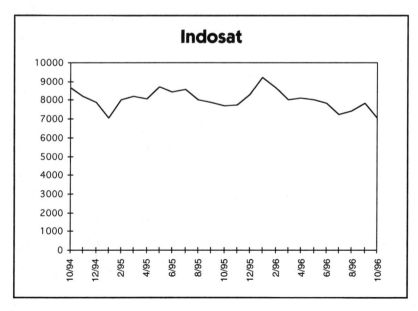

9

Investing Abroad: Going Where the Growth Is

The Growing Global Marketplace Trend

As the world's economy gets bigger, the United States' share in it is becoming smaller. More and more, the fastest-growing stocks and the highest-yielding bonds and certificates of deposit are turning up not in this country but overseas.

How the World Is Changing

In 1970, the worldwide gross product was slightly more than $2 trillion. Of that, the United States contributed almost half. In 1992, the world was producing goods and services each year worth $18 trillion, more than nine times the 1970 figure, with the United States contributing about a third. At the same rate of growth, the world could greet the year 2000 with its economy measurable at more than $50 trillion, with the United States' share kicking in somewhat less than 25 percent.

There are many reasons to think that the world's economy will enjoy an even faster rate of growth as we move toward the year 2000. For example, every week brings new technological developments that enable us to research, calculate, devise, produce, and communicate at a rate and to an extent that only a few years ago would have been considered science fiction. In addition, international cooperation to limit the dangers of war, to stabilize currencies, to ensure health, to universalize education, to protect real and intellectual property, and to keep open the lines of communication and trade between formerly remote parts of the world has reached an impressive level of success.

Another reason to be optimistic about the future of the world's economy is the number of economically emerging countries that are committed to sharing in the world's wealth. These countries now offer energies, resources, and skills they once seemed unable or disinclined to share.

Manmohan Singh, India's minister of finance, put it this way: "India is a new ball game. Our country is now prepared for big changes [in order to prosper]." Other formerly impoverished countries that have embraced economic reform, according to the World Bank, include the Czech Republic, Chile, Ghana, Indonesia, Morocco, Poland, South Korea, and Turkey. Their rising economies are a magnet for foreign investment. In time, they may present attractive markets for other countries' goods, providing another thrust to a larger world economy by 2000.

Where the Most Attractive Stocks Are Traded

The world's largest companies—Fiat, Hoeschst, Nestlé, Philips, Sony, Suzuki, Unilever, and those with other well-known names—keep growing, spreading their influence worldwide, and predictably raising their dividends. As a result, they are the kinds of companies into which prudent investors like to put their money. Yet, of the world's 100 largest corporations, only 28 percent are based in the United States. The shares of the remaining 72 percent are traded on stock exchanges located far from Wall Street.

In 1970, the U.S. stock exchanges dominated the world, representing 66 percent of its total market capitalization.

Today, their share is less than 40 percent. In the same period, Japan went from 15 percent of the world's market capitalization to a share rivaling ours. The Tokyos of the future are soaring fast. The hot stocks are, more and more, traded in Bangkok, Jakarta, Kuala Lumpur, Istanbul, Sao Paulo, Singapore, and Warsaw; fewer are traded on Wall Street.

According to Morgan Stanley, since 1970, the United States market has been ranked among the top five returning markets only four times, and it has not been the top performing market once. In that same time, Hong Kong has been in the top five 13 times, and the combined Singapore/Malaysia index 11 times. This helps to explain why advisers to U.S.-based pension and investment trusts—among the largest investors in the world— are urging their clients to invest more overseas. You can do the same. If you remain solely in the U.S. stock market, you not only deprive yourself of most of the world's investments, you also give up a shot at the fastest growing issues.

A Booming World Economy

The emerging markets are growing so fast it is a full-time job just keeping track of their growth. In China, there are now more than 13,000 share-holding companies, and the number is soaring upward by around 40 percent each year. Although relatively few of these companies are listed on the major Chinese exchanges, this will change as the exchanges improve and mature. Within the next 20 years, the stock exchanges at Shanghai or Shenzhen could be among the world's top five stock markets.

The "established" stock markets of the emerging world also have much room to grow. The Hong Kong stock market, for example, has soared. In 1964, Hong Kong's Hang Seng Index had a value of 100; it now trades at a value of more than 13,000. Its market capitalization—the total value of all the securities traded on it—is growing by 100 percent a year. These soaring percentages are not surprising considering that the Hong Kong market started at such low levels compared to the older established markets.

Emerging Means Profitable

During 1996, the top five emerging markets returned the following in dollar terms:

Country	Percentage of Return in Dollar Terms
Russia	+143
Venezuela	+97
Poland	+62
Brazil	+53
China "B"	+41

The top five stock markets of the older established economies performed as follows over the same period:

Finland	+38
Sweden	+31
Spain	+31
Ireland	+28
Portugal	+28

The disparity between the performance of developed and emerging markets is explained by the fact that the world's manufacturing base is shifting to countries and to markets with far lower costs than those of the established economies. Compare the top-ranked emerging market of Russia to the top-ranked established market of Finland and you'll see what I mean. Because it has been so low for so long, the Russian market could rise 150 percent in one year and still have room to grow.

As an investor, how well would you have been rewarded by Russia's 150 percent rise? An investment of $10,000 would have grown to $25,000 in just more than a year.

A Winner in Warsaw

Poland, like Hungary and the Czech Republic, was a thriving market economy before the Communists took over 50 years ago. Since Poland was freed from communism in the late 1980s, it has been transforming itself from a Soviet satellite to a market economy. Poland's strategy for this transformation has been to privatize many of the state-owned companies and to distribute shares in them to the Polish people. The rationale for this strategy is to give Poles a stake in the success of their market economy; in effect, to tie their well-being to the well-being of the Polish economy.

And that economy has performed very well. In 1993, the total economy grew by 4 percent and industrial production grew by more than 8 percent. Most of the economies of Western Europe were lucky to grow at all during 1993. For example, Holland, which grew the most, did so by only 2 percent and the economy of Germany shrank by 1.4 percent and that of France by 1.2 percent. All the other economies in the old Eastern bloc shrank as well.

It is unusual to have the type of growth Poland has experienced combined with essential stability. It happened because the strategy of wide distribution of shares in Polish companies has created a very large—and loyal—domestic market. Unlike so many "emerging markets," the foreign participation in the Polish stock market was very small compared to the local participation. In 1993, only 20 percent of all security orders were placed by foreigners. This is good news for any small market and gives it an enviable stability.

Poland's stock market is miles ahead of the stock markets of most other emerging markets in that it has an independent securities commission that maintains reliability, efficiency, and honesty in the market—and that market is poised to expand. There are currently hundreds of firms waiting to be privatized.

My job is to anticipate when the stock market of an entire country will rise strongly. What I've seen over the years is that you can get very solid growth by buying the stocks of established blue chips that are heavily involved in the economies of emerging markets, like Poland's. In general, a country's rising stock market often indicates that the country is getting richer. And a growing economy benefits from the types of companies discussed in the following sections.

Unilever

One way to prosper from the economic growth of emerging markets like Poland is to buy stock in Unilever. Unilever is the consumer products company that owns such brands as Lipton

Tea, Birds Eye, All detergent, Dove, Vaseline, Pepsodent, Surf, Wisk, Popsicle, Mrs. Butterworth's, Calvin Klein, Elizabeth Arden, and Fabergé. Successful blue chips such as Unilever acquire other companies that make products they believe will appeal to consumers. In fact, Unilever has, at times, acquired companies at the rate of one per week.

Unilever is owned 50-50 by an English company and a Dutch company, with each parent company operating under the direction of the same board of directors. Unilever is well established in Europe and is superbly placed to move into the booming Central European economies. It was one of the first large Western consumer products firms to go into the new Poland in a big way. Its most important acquisition was the main Polish detergent maker, now called Lever Polska. This acquisition was a natural for Unilever because 100 years ago, the Lever Brothers came out with the world's first brand of packaged laundry soap. Besides Poland, Unilever is expanding into Hungary and the Czech Republic. Its sales to this region alone are doubling every year.

Today, besides selling detergent to emerging markets, Unilever is also selling disposable diapers. In a joint venture with Kimberly-Clark, Unilever is producing and marketing diapers in India. With its poor, but emerging, economy, India is—after China—the second most populous country in the world. With an annual birth rate of 28 million babies, India, by 2000, is likely to have millions of babies wearing Unilever diapers.

Through its Fabergé company, Unilever markets Fendi, Lagerfeld, and Chloé perfumes, which are likely to be sought after by the women in emerging economies as they grow in wealth. And, in another joint venture with Pepsi, Unilever is creating new tea drinks to be marketed through Pepsi's huge global distribution network.

In sum, Unilever is perfectly positioned to benefit from emerging markets. Virtually every demographic group, as it gains disposable income, becomes a consumer of one or more Unilever-owned brands.

Unilever's stock price has risen steadily for most of the past 20 years, soaring to a new high every year, yet its price-earnings ratio of about 13 is unbelievably low. A tried-and-true blue chip that is right on the pulse of the world's hottest growing economies, Unilever's stock should be in your investment portfolio.

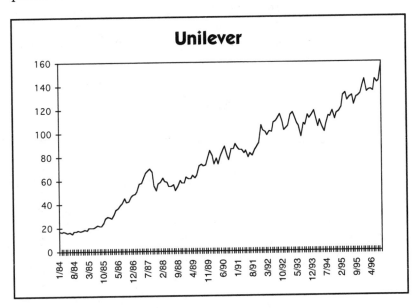

Nestlé

As the world's largest food and nonalcoholic beverage group, Nestlé's name is recognized around the globe. Yet few people fully realize the extent of Nestlé's presence in emerging markets. Nestlé operates 489 factories in 69 countries, with products sold in more than 100 countries. Nearly 40 percent of Nestlé's factories are located in the emerging markets of the Asia/Pacific region, Africa, Latin America, and Eastern Europe. More than 30 percent of its operating profits are currently derived from these markets, a portion that is expected to steadily increase.

Nestlé has been in the Asia/Pacific region almost since its inception in 1867. The company is well known and admired for its ability to use its knowledgeable and experienced management, and its long-term commitment and excellent reputation allow for advantages when negotiating new contracts or building new factories in emerging markets. By entering these emerging markets early and catering to local market character-istics and preferences, Nestlé is able to establish a strong and enduring market position.

Nestlé is sometimes undervalued by the market. This usu-ally doesn't last long, and its stock price usually rises to its true value. If you can catch Nestlé stock during such an underval-ued period, buy it.

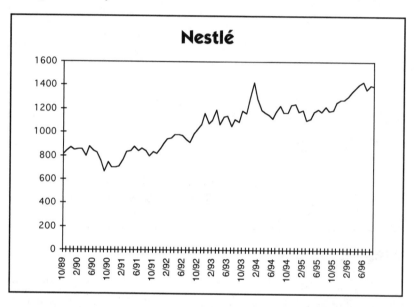

Suzuki

While much of the Japanese market remains far below its 1989 highs, Suzuki Motor Company has been a steady riser for the past five years. In June 1996 it reached its all-time high.

Suzuki's marketing strategy is simple but effective. It tar-gets emerging markets with big populations in which to sell its well-made small cars and motorcycles, usually by forming a partnership with a local company to help with its marketing. Suzuki uses this partnership approach in developed countries as well. For example, General Motors owns 5 percent of Suzuki and, through a Canadian joint venture, sells such Suzuki cars as Geo Metro, Spring, and Tracer. Under its own name, Suzuki sells the Swift, Samurai, and Sidekick in North America.

In the future, Suzuki's big growth is likely to come from emerging market countries. In India and Hungary for example, demand is thriving and local manufacturing plants are running at full capacity!

In its Japanese home market, Suzuki has been the leading mini-car producer for about 20 years, and it is the third largest worldwide manufacturer of motorcycles (after Honda and Yamaha), with mopeds making up 80 percent of these sales.

The stagnant Japanese auto market in 1994 didn't hurt Suzuki because it specializes in small, low-cost vehicles. Even the global recession coupled with the high yen has not adversely affected its sales. On a PE ratio, Suzuki is the cheapest automaker in Japan. The PE ratio depends on what the total earnings happen to be at any given time, divided by the total value of shares at that time. The general Nikkei Index currently sells at 69 times earnings. The Japanese NRI 400 sector is broken down into 21 categories, including one for automobiles and auto parts. This category had an average PE ratio of 28 for December 1995 to December 1996. Suzuki has a PE ratio of 21.

This has been good for Suzuki's stock price. When the Nikkei was at its all-time high in late 1989, Suzuki was at 1,000 yen per share. But in U.S. dollars, because the yen was 145 to the dollar, the price was $6.90 per share. When the Nikkei was down by more than 40 percent from its 1989 peaks, Suzuki hit a new record, reaching 1,400 yen. Because the yen then was worth 105 per dollar, Suzuki's price per share equaled $13.33. This means that in dollar terms, the price was 93 percent higher than it was before the Japanese stock crash.

This highlights another important reason for investing abroad. The best stocks are denominated in currencies that are strong against the dollar, so you can make money even if the stock price falls in local terms.

As of 1996, Suzuki had factories in 29 countries, including Indonesia, Pakistan, Spain, Taiwan, and Thailand, in addition to the countries discussed earlier. Suzuki opened a car factory in Hungary in 1993. At a quarter billion dollars, it is the largest Japanese investment in Eastern Europe. As part of the process of getting the factory up and running, Hungarian workers were flown to Japan for training in the Japanese way of making cars.

The differences between the cultures of these two countries will mean a big change for the Hungarians from their former Communist ways of operating a factory.

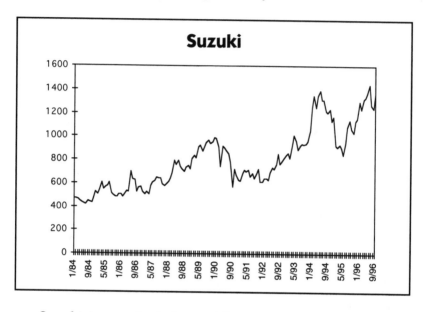

Suzuki is my single best pick among Japanese stocks. It combines the best about Japan—efficiency and high currency value—with the best of the emerging economy. As long as the emerging markets boom, so will Suzuki.

Singapore Airlines

There is a man in Florida who may have accumulated the world's most frequent flyer miles. With six million miles on Delta and hundreds of thousands of miles on most other major U.S. airlines, he can take 300 round-trip flights free. He has been nearly everywhere in the world and has flown most of the world's more than 50 major airlines. Which is his favorite? Singapore Airlines.

On a small island surrounded by Malaysia and Indonesia, Singapore is an economic powerhouse. With less than three million people, it has a huge place in the burgeoning new economy of East Asia. The manufacturing base of the world is shifting to this region, and Singapore is at the center of it, not only as the financial capital but as the transportation hub as well.

While the U.S. airline industry has lost billions since 1991, Singapore Air—based on a Singapore exchange of $6.93— made $700 million in 1996 alone. In fact, since 1991, it has been the world's most profitable airline.

Anyone who has flown Singapore Air can tell you the reasons for its success. It is superbly run and staffed by employees for whom service with a genuine smile is not just a memory from the 1950s. In addition, Singapore Air has the youngest and most efficient fleet of planes in the world, with the world's most efficient airport (Singapore) as its hub. Its planes go to every growing part of Asia. When, for example, a new area of China begins to boom, Singapore Air requests new routes.

Singapore Air's balance sheet is in enviable shape, and its stock is clearly undervalued. It holds S$54 million in cash, and has a proven management, an excellent geo-economic route system, and top-rate equipment. It also has increasing dividends and a stock price of nine times earnings. Compare that to American Airlines, which has lost hundreds of millions since 1992, or with United Airlines, which has lost over half a billion dollars, also since 1992.

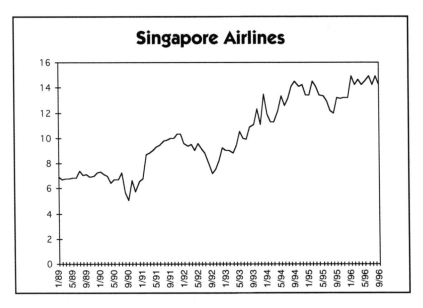

As Singapore's biggest private employer (one of every 74 workers is a Singapore Air employee), and with the single largest capitalization of any stock on the Singapore exchange, Singapore Air faces the danger of becoming a victim of its own success. Protectionist sentiments in other countries could be obstacles the airline will have to surmount.

This may not be a problem for Singapore Air. As it moves to become a global player, it has begun forming alliances with other airlines. It has two already: with Delta and Swiss Air, and it plans to purchase 25 percent of the stock in Australia's Qantas Ansett airlines.

Singapore Air is on the move. Over the long term, I predict it will be a winner.

10

The Falling Dollar: Turning It to Your Advantage

The Falling Dollar Trend

Two fundamental measures of any nation's economic virility are its currency and its stock market. Judging by these standards, the United States' economy has given a fine downward spiral performance. The U.S. dollar continues to fall against most other strong currencies and the U.S. stock market, although fairly steady, has been outperformed by many other world markets. Unless the U.S. government tackles our economic problems at the roots, it might as well drive the last nail into its briefcase. Unfortunately, the denial of a Balanced Budget Amendment potentially sealed the fate of the doomed dollar. American investors who want to see their capital value truly grow should consider buying foreign currencies; otherwise, their reserves are likely to deflate right along with the greenback.

The shocking fact is that, since 1970, the U.S. dollar has lost more than 75 percent of its value against the strongest world currencies. Some will argue that the U.S. hasn't fallen so much but that other countries are getting stronger and rising faster than the U.S. is. That may be true, but, as Americans have watched these economies grow, they have done nothing to improve their own. Participation in globalization, which can open vast opportunities if fully embraced, seems to utterly confuse our regressive governing body. Until the U.S. Congress decides to acknowledge its mistakes and follow the economic example set by other thriving nations, better returns will be available in stronger instruments outside the U.S. dollar.

Why the U.S. Dollar Is Weak

To understand why the dollar is not stronger, we must take a brief look at U.S. policy and how it has historically encouraged the dollar's declining value. Basically, maintaining a weak dollar has become a U.S. government priority. The dollar represented a fixed unit of gold and had a tangible value until 1913, when the Federal Reserve Act established a paper monopoly money with the dollar being pegged to gold and convertible whenever the holder desired. Beginning in 1934, however, citizens could no longer convert their money to a fixed amount of gold, nor could they purchase gold. This restriction forced Americans to hold on to their dollars. At the same time, however, under the terms of the Bretton Woods agreement, foreign central banks could still convert their U.S. dollars into gold.

In the late 1960s, the U.S. government felt free to expand the money supply without concern, inflating and devaluing the dollar based upon a "gentleman's agreement" with central banks asking them not to withdraw gold for dollars. But in 1971, the central banks of the world recognized that the United States had no plans of maintaining the dollar's value, rather, just the opposite, and they were not willing to cooperate any longer. They began withdrawing massive amounts of gold to protect their investments and consequently prompted the U.S. government to renege their offer of gold for dollars and to ultimately withdraw from Bretton Woods.

Thus, the last remnant of discipline connecting the dollar to gold and real value was gone. From that point, the dollar has been pure "fiat money," useful only because the government has designated it "legal tender," but having no other basis of value. The results since that time make the plight of the dollar obvious: the question is not whether it will go down, but by how much and how fast.

An Example Shows the Dollar's Devaluation

To fully appreciate the devaluation of the U.S. currency, you must try to experience its impact firsthand. Imagine that you and a Japanese businessman are standing in front of a building somewhere in the United States. The building is for sale at a price of $30 million. You both saw the same building in 1970, when the price was only $10 million. Today, at triple its former price, you are not interested in buying the building. To you, it's no bargain. But to the Japanese businessman, it is.

In 1970, when the price was $10 million, the Japanese businessman would have had to spend 3.57 billion yen (or $10 million in U.S. dollars) to buy it. Now, the price of the building has risen in dollar terms, but not in yen. At the December 1996 rate of exchange, $30 million translates into 3.39 billion yen. For the Japanese businessman, the price hasn't tripled, it has fallen by 5 percent. So, naturally, the Japanese man says, "I'll buy it." And you, with weaker dollars, turn it down.

The same situation applies for a German businessman or anyone who holds German marks, and also for Swiss franc holders. In fact, in 1992, a Swiss would have been able to buy the building for 13 percent less than a quarter of a century ago. The U.S. dollar has, against the Swiss franc, been locked in a downward spiral for the past 25 years. Its decline in value has been long and painful; the corrections upward have been short and weak.

We Americans are dismayed to see how cheaply foreigners (using their strong currency) can buy U.S. companies or properties, especially when we realize that we can no longer afford them, simply because our currency is so weak. The picture gets even worse when you consider how the incomes of the Japanese, Germans, and Swiss have been rising compared to

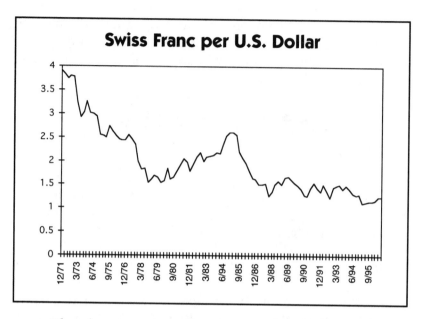

ours. They have consistently produced high demand export goods at affordable prices; consequently, their economies have risen and so have their incomes.

The Japanese businessman who can buy the office building in 1996 for less than he would have paid 26 years earlier probably has more money to spend on real estate investments than he had in 1970. After all, as his currency got stronger, he saved a lot in those 25 years and has more money to spend on buildings than the comparable U.S. businessman. In other words, many more Japanese have 3.39 billion yen to spend in 1996 than had 3.57 billion yen to spend in 1970.

The U.S. businessman had the opposite experience. As the dollar kept going down in value, he could see his cost of living going up and his bank account rising slower than the cost of the things he wanted to buy. So, he put off buying; he had to. For him, with less to spend and with little enthusiasm for buying, the price of the building had tripled. For the Japanese businessman, who had become more prosperous and could easily have spent more, the price had dropped substantially.

When you realize that, since 1970, the incomes of most Germans, Japanese, and Swiss (and others holding strong currencies) have risen tremendously just in terms of their own marks, yen, and francs, the decline of U.S. living standards becomes even more noticeable. Since the Japanese business-man is earning more in 1996 than he was in 1970, you could say he has to work less (maybe half as much) to earn the 3.39 billion yen needed to buy the building. So, instead of the price going down 5 percent for him in 26 years, it actually went down even more in labor terms. In other words, for him, the building became more than 5 percent cheaper. For the U.S. businessman, the price of the building seemed to triple, but in terms of labor needed to earn the dollars to buy it, the price he would have to pay was even higher.

The Dollar Just Continues to Fall

The path of the dollar has been unaffected by the growth and decline of other world markets; it has continued to fall. There has been no logical pattern or reason for its decline; the dollar just continues to fall. For example, in relation to Japan, the dollar has fallen when the Japanese stock market soared, when it plunged, and when it rallied; it has also fallen when Japan's economy looked stronger than the United States' as well as when it looked weaker than the United States'.

Domestically, the cycle is no different. When Wall Street soared from 1985 to 1987, the dollar fell. When Wall Street collapsed in October 1987, the dollar fell. Wall Street recovered, the dollar fell. Wall Street fell again, and so did the dollar. When the U.S. trade deficit rose, the dollar fell; the trade deficit fell, so did the dollar. When the unification of Germany was announced, an event that should have caused a heavy drain on marks from West to East Germany, the mark was expected to fall against the dollar. Instead, the mark rose to a record high, and the dollar fell.

More worrisome than all these examples is the fact that as war broke out in the Middle East in 1990, the dollar was not viewed as the safe haven for the world's money as it had been in previous wars; in other words, the dollar no longer lived up to historical standards. It fell again. The Swiss franc and the Japanese yen, currencies of two non-oil-producing countries, rose instead when the world's oil reserves were threatened. The currency of the United States, with its comparatively rich oil reserves, fell. This situation puzzled even currency experts at the time. Just when the dollar had fallen so much that they thought it was due for a bounce, it fell again. The rebound didn't come until about eight months later, and when it did, it bounced like a dead cat.

The dollar took a huge plunge in the late 1980s and struggled unsuccessfully to get back on its feet. Each time the greenback tried to rise, it got only so far before it was beaten back to new lows. The dollar has not only fallen against established European currencies, but also against the major economies of the Asian Pacific—Japan, Singapore, and Malaysia. Against these currencies, the dollar has recently reached new lows.

To understand why the dollar keeps falling, it is useful for Americans to take a good hard look at themselves. A nation is generally comprised of extremely diverse groups of people. On a broad, objective scale, as when viewed by foreigners, it takes on a single personality. For example, the world thinks of Japanese people as one type and Germans as another, and so on. Americans are often perceived as lazy, rich, and spoiled, living off a rapidly diminishing trust fund and refusing to do what is necessary to provide for a secure future. Many individuals do not fit that picture and may have hard-earned money that they want to protect. However, as long as these assets are denominated in dollars, they may have labored largely in vain.

A majority of America's wealth, whether it is tied up in real estate, securities, or certificates of deposit, is reckoned in dollars, the declining currency of a nation that is eating its seed capital; its savings are in the currency of a country that refuses to save and simply pushes its unpaid debts into its children's hands. That is how the world sees us, as debtors with a declining economy, and it continues to give less for our dollars.

It is possible, and now very easy, to move money into stronger currencies. Instead of holding Japanese or Swiss currency, which is not the best way to protect investment value, today's investor should consider buying the interest-bearing government bonds of selected countries—an easier and more profitable move.

Despite the gloomy portrayal of the dollar thus far, in the past 25 years or so, the U.S. dollar has not fallen against all the world's 175 different currencies. Since 1970, it has risen against most of them. From 1970 to 1990, only 36 currencies have risen against the dollar, and of those 36, only 16 rose in value more than 25 percent. Five currencies doubled (or more) in value against the dollar during the past 25 years, a disastrous period for the greenback. Still, as the most powerful nation in the world, we need to reform our dismal dollar.

Profitable Foreign Investments for Americans

Pure currency comparison does not take interest rates into consideration, especially compounded rates that can boost gains simply from exchange rate moves. For example, if someone gave you 100 Swiss francs in 1970 and you held them in your pocket, after 26 years, you would still have 100 Swiss francs. However, if you had deposited that money (US$23.20) in a bank that paid 3 percent interest compounding annually, after 26 years you would have 215.66 francs or US$183.83, a 692.33 percent return in U.S. dollar terms. Bonds, especially zero coupon bonds, make excellent tools for safe investment and compound interest earnings by providing an investment in an economy rather than a straight monetary exchange. The following currencies have proven themselves as profitable investment tools for Americans in the past 25 years:

Currency	Rise in Value (12-31-69 to 3-30-95)
Swiss franc	+267.4%
Japanese yen	+298.8%
German mark	+160.6%
Austrian schilling	+160.5%
Dutch guilder	+128.7%

Ideally, when you buy a foreign bond, you would like to be getting a rising currency, a high-interest yield, and a potential decline in interest rates, which increases the bond price. As of 1996, yen bonds didn't meet these criteria, although in a few years they might. Three time-tested government bonds that do meet the criteria are German, Swiss, and Dutch. (The Austrian schilling is not a widely traded currency, and since it is tied to the German mark, buying German government bonds would give you all the advantages you'd get from Austrian bonds.) For each currency, values can be expected to rise, current yields are healthy, and there is a probability that rates will fall, pushing bond prices higher.

Swiss Franc

No currency has held its value over the past 150 years better than the Swiss franc. The modern Swiss franc was born in 1850—two years after the Swiss Constitution put an end to cantons using their own currencies—and it was declared equal to the French franc, each being defined as 4.5 grams of fine silver.

Since then, it is interesting to see how those three values have held up. Today, it takes about four French francs to equal one Swiss franc, yet the Swiss franc has held its value in terms of silver. Most currencies have lost a great amount of value against silver over the past century. Italy's lira, for example, has lost 99.9 percent of its silver value since 1862, when it was also fixed at 4.5 grams of silver. With silver prices at $5.50 per ounce, 4.5 grams of silver would now be worth about US$.80, which is what the Swiss franc is worth in dollar terms. In short, while other currencies have faded against silver, the Swiss franc has held its own.

Over time, paper currencies tend to lose value against commodities like silver. All currencies were once freely convertible into specific weights or amounts of gold or silver, but none has held its value so well against its original measure as the Swiss franc.

In comparison, the 1850 U.S. dollar was equal to 24.06 grams of silver (about three-quarters of an ounce). Today, at $5 an ounce, 24.06 grams of silver are worth $3.88. In other words, it would take $3.88 to buy the same amount of silver that $.58 would have bought in 1850. Seen this way, the dollar has lost more than 85 percent of its value, while the Swiss franc has held value over the same period measured against the same unchanging commodity—silver—by which both were first defined.

Monetary stability rarely exists without political and economic stability, and that of the Swiss is unparalleled around the world. For instance, Swiss voters have held the four main political parties in nearly perfect equilibrium for more than 70 years. Unlike other nations, in Switzerland ultimate sovereignty rests with the people. Specifically, power resides in the local neighborhoods where free citizens are most able to control their lives. It stands to reason that the more power individuals have over their own lives, the more incentive they have to keep their country free, stable, and prosperous.

Accordingly, the most basic unit of Swiss political life—the unit from which all else flows—is the local community government called the *gemeindeversammlung*. In English, "municipality" comes close to capturing what *gemeinde* means, but perhaps the best approximation is the old-fashioned New England "town meeting," where citizens assembled to decide the pressing questions facing their town. The gemeindeversammlung, however, is far more potent and universal than the New England town meeting. One becomes a Swiss citizen only by first becoming a citizen of a gemeinde. On all Swiss passports and official personal papers, the name of the gemeinde is prominent. What is unusual is that this town could well be one that neither the citizen nor the past few generations of his or her family have ever seen. Citizenship in a gemeinde stays with a family and its descendants even if they no longer live there. The allegiance, however, remains strong. When the Swiss are asked where they are from, most will answer with their gemeinde even though they may have never been there.

At last count, there were 3,072 Swiss gemeinde for roughly 6.4 million Swiss. This averages some 2,000 Swiss per gemeinde, which vary greatly in size (for example, some may have as few as 12 people, while Zurich has 370,000). The existence of so many self-governing communities allows Swiss citizens to vent their frustrations among neighbors. Some communities may be avidly liberal and others extremely conservative, yet each can exist in its own area where its own prejudices can be aired without the fear that the prejudices of other communities will disrupt its way of life.

It is likely that this strict decentralization and compartmentalization keep Switzerland stable and unified in a way that other more centralized countries are not. Because each citizen is responsible to his gemeinde even though he may not live there, his interests to keep it productive and healthy are as strong as those toward his actual home town. (If U.S. residents were held responsible for more than their own interests, our domestic policy might be very different. For instance, Proposition 187 and U.S.-Cuban relations might be handled very differently!) However else each gemeinde or canton may differ from the others, they all retain their essential "Swissness"—that policy of respect for others that results in strength through diversity.

Like its political system, Swiss government bonds are the most secure and financially reliable of any in the world. That is because the Swiss government is the most financially responsible. These bonds should be a part of any investment portfolio.

German Mark

When Germans think about their currency, one specter lurks near the surface of their minds: that of the runaway inflation that once devastated the German economy. From 1920 to 1923, the German mark collapsed in the most bizarre hyperinflation of all time. It is hard to find terms appropriate to describe the collapse of the mark some 70 years ago. Savings accounts that would have let one retire in style in 1914 could not even buy a third-class postage stamp a few years later. In 1914, one U.S. dollar bought 4.2 marks; in late 1923, one dollar bought 4.2 trillion. The mark actually fell further, but by then no one bothered to measure its exact value. In fact, it no longer carried any value, and as a result the German economy engaged in a different form of exchange: barter.

A new currency, the reichsmark, was established in 1924 at the rate of one trillion old marks for one new reichsmark. This was to be Adolf Hitler's currency, and not surprisingly, he used the most barbaric methods in modern history to keep it from losing value. After Hitler came to power in 1933, marks were sent out of the country, usually to Switzerland. This dramatic outflow began to depress the new mark's value, so Hitler declared a moratorium on all mark outflows in 1934. Even strict jail sentences were not enough deterrent and marks continued to leave. On December 1, 1936, the death penalty was imposed for sending marks out of the country. Despite these harsh restrictions, the mark continued to fall and when Hitler's reign finally collapsed, the reichsmark lost virtually all its purchasing power. For the second time in 23 years, Germans saw their currency become worthless.

The Germans vowed that this humiliation would never happen again. Backed by U.S. capital, the deutsch mark we know today was born on June 20, 1948. The D-mark was launched with high hopes, but it soon began to lose value. From its original 1948 value of DM3.33 per dollar, the value slid a year later to DM4.2 per dollar and fell to an all-time low of DM8.06 per dollar in 1951 (that is, each mark was worth 12.4 cents). It had lost 59 percent of its value in just three years, but that was the end. Over the next 40 years, Germany's "economic miracle" did not stop and from its low point in 1951 to its value today, the mark has risen 460 percent against the dollar.

The Germans' resolve to keep the mark strong is easily understood and can be greatly beneficial to outside investors. Any time you can buy German mark bonds during a period of temporary mark weakness you should, because it is not likely to remain weak for long and you would probably earn a nice

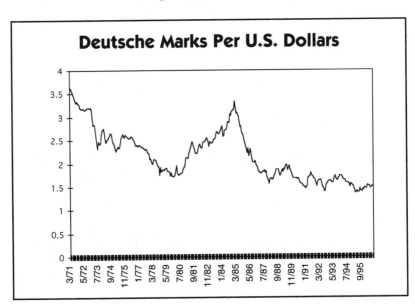

Deutsche Marks Per U.S. Dollars

return, recently in the 6 to 7 percent range. Also, as German interest rates fall, the bond prices will rise making for a great overall investment.

Just as American memories are haunted by the economic nightmare of the Great Depression, Germans are still haunted by the runaway inflation that destroyed their currency and the fortunes of millions of families. It is not surprising that protecting the mark has been the national priority for decades. The German bank, the Bundesbank, has a legal duty to defend the mark, and it takes that duty very seriously.

Dutch Guilder

The Dutch guilder holds the world's record for stability, stretching back almost 400 years. In 1587, the Bank of Venice launched an innovative monetary campaign in the Western world. Just as Florence had previously introduced the world to banking, neighboring Venice introduced it to bank notes. Similar paper money had once been used in ancient China, where it became worthless due to inflation, but this was its first appearance in the West. Its success was short-lived in Venice, but elsewhere persevered. In 1609, Amsterdam began issuing what is now the world's oldest paper currency.

Holland's paper guilder was not inflated. Each paper guilder was essentially a warehouse receipt representing a fixed weight of metal at the bank. Everyone knew the paper guilder issued by the Bank of Amsterdam was as good as gold, and it was much easier to carry than a sack of coins. In fact, so sought after was the currency for just this convenience that from 1609 to 1794, the paper money basically traded at a 3 to 9 percent premium over the gold content.

The Dutch guilder suffered as a result of the 1794 French invasion, but began to rebound after Waterloo in 1815 and remained steady until Hitler's invasion in 1940. After World War II, the guilder proved to be incredibly elastic and recovered ten years earlier than the German mark. The mark and the guilder were the first currencies to show that there could be stability among the major European monetary systems; they also showed that strong European currencies could act as a stable block against the gyrating U.S. dollar. Since 1980, the guilder has remained steady at almost 90 percent of the mark's value.

A common belief among investors is that a big fall in a country's interest rate automatically triggers a fall in the currency's price. However, the path of the Dutch guilder from 1985 to 1988 illustrated a contrary action. During that time, deposit rates on the guilder fell by half, from 8 to 4 percent, yet the guilder doubled in value against the dollar, going from 27 cents to 55 cents.

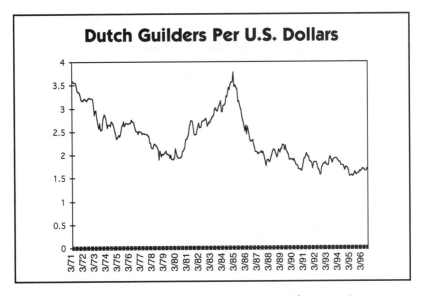

The guilder is a competitive currency that is often overlooked. It currently has a longer record of strength and stability than any other currency. In a few years, the paper Dutch guilder will celebrate its 400th birthday. With bond yields up again, the 1990s are a good time to own Dutch bonds.

French Franc

Aside from Italy with its lira, few nations have so transformed themselves and their currencies in the past few years more than France. Not long ago, it was viewed as a place heavy on charm, but short on efficiency and cursed with what seemed to be an eternally sick currency. Today, it still has the style and charm it always had, but in some ways has become more efficient than Germany.

Who would have believed 15 years ago that France would one day have a lower inflation rate, a stronger currency, and more profitable government bonds than Germany has? Who would have guessed that today the French would enjoy faster, safer, and more punctual trains and a superior overall telephone system than the Germans do? All this is true.

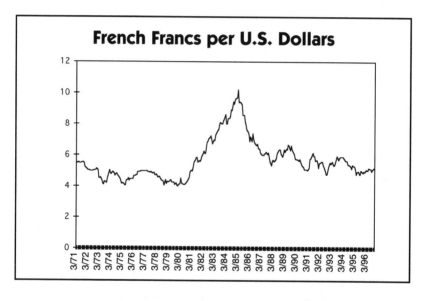

You can compare France's changes to the changes in Italy. In one vital way, France's progress has been better. All of France's regions have participated in its betterment, unlike vast parts of southern Italy, which cannot shake the past. French inflation is about 2 percent. Bond yields are much higher, in the 6 to 8 percent range. The franc itself has been steady for more than 30 years, and it has sometimes risen in foreign exchange markets even faster than the mark. French franc bonds are a rare example of an investment where yields are high and inflation is low, with a good record of overall stability.

Bonds That Offer Higher Yields in Weaker Currencies

The last two bonds we'll look at offer much higher yields—in double digits—but pay them in currencies that are not as strong as the others discussed in this chapter. Italian yields, for example, have been in the double digits for years.

Italian Lira

Recently, an extraordinary thing has been happening in Italy. For the first time, there is wide support for measures that would put Italy's financial house in order. Inflation has come down, and the big budget deficit is now under attack. The big outcry over official corruption shows that Italians are sick of "business as usual." As a result, foreign capital has begun to rediscover Italy. The lira has stabilized, and I believe interest rates will drop much more. Italian inflation is around 4 percent, which means bonds are paying a high real rate of return of 5.5 percent. You don't often find this happening. If you are willing to take the currency risk, this bond could provide an exceptional return over the next few years.

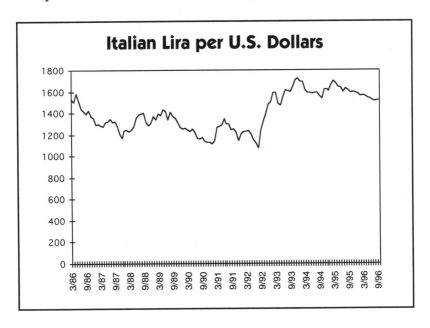

Spanish Peseta

Spain's story is similar to that of Italy. Inflation is 4.5 percent, but unemployment is more than 20 percent. Interest rates are near double digits, which means that real rates, after deducting for inflation, are quite high. Rates will have to drop to deal with the slow Spanish economy, so besides getting high current yields, chances are that your bonds will rise in price. The only question is the peseta. It has fallen in the past and returns will vary depending on the amount of future devaluation.

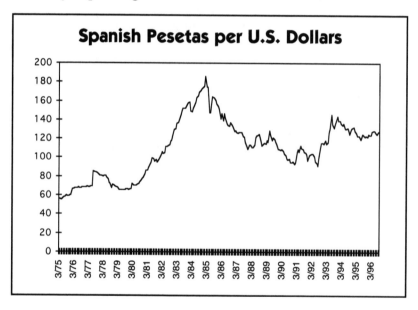

Spanish Pesetas per U.S. Dollars

A Final Note

So there you have five bonds offering diversity. Plan on spending about $10,000 a piece for them. If you don't want to buy all five, you could choose one or two. Depending on your investment desires, you may want to stick to the more conservative bonds, or you may want to be more aggressive by pursuing the higher yields of Italy or Spain.

The falling dollar does help some U.S. companies. Those like Caterpillar, John Deere, Boeing, and ADM for example will profit more as the dollar falls and products made in the United

dustrial Revolution hit. They are not hampered by precon-
ived ideas of what they can and cannot do and have no fear
moving forward; therefore, the growth potential of
igapore and Malaysia seems unlimited. Historically, soci-
es with this rare combination of characteristics have been
ose most likely to prosper.

ell-Performing Asian Economies

In Malaysia and Singapore, economic wisdom differs from
at in the United States, where an announcement that jobs
ve been created and economic growth is up sends financial
alysts, bond traders, and markets out the window. Once,
ws of more and better jobs was greeted with joy and opti-
sm by American investors, not with the fear that interest
es would rise and the economy would slow down. Joy and
timism, however, greet such news in Malaysia, Singapore,
d Asia in general, where people live by the wise proverb:
lake hay while the sun shines." Those countries worry little
out inflation; instead, they concentrate on economic growth.

Proof, they say, lies in the pudding, and Singapore's econ-
iy grew at an astounding 7 percent annual rate during most
1996, outperforming even the most optimistic estimates.
rprisingly, interest rates there still remain low—lower now
n U.S. rates. In fact, interest rates are moderate in the fastest
owing Asian countries, enabling them to sustain high levels
economic growth. Contrary to popular American beliefs,
v interest rates have not stopped currencies from rising.
an's interest rates are now close to 3 percent, although the
i's performance has been extremely strong, especially
iinst the dollar. Clearly, this is evidence that strong growth
economies does not have to mean trouble in the form of
her interest rates, and that low interest rates do not neces-
ily make the currency undesirable for investors.

rong Morals Bind Cultures

Backing up the superbly performing economies of Asia is a
ing moral glue that binds the cultures of its nations. In
aysia and Singapore, honesty and respect play a profound

States become even cheaper. More important, they make good
products that emerging economies need. This is a great recipe
for growth. Be on the lookout for companies with this combination and, along with foreign bonds, you can turn a falling
dollar to your advantage.

*Special thanks to Chris Weber for his invaluable contribution to
this chapter; specifically, his knowledge of historical data and relative
performance of the dollar versus other currencies.*

11

Investing in th
Companies of A
Booming Econon

The Manufacturing Tren

The greatest positive impact of the world's sh
facturing base is occurring in Southeast Asia wh
economies are booming due to the overwhelming
their products. Worldwide, Singapore and Mala
economies that are consistently growing the fast
showing spectacular economic growth and each
in-depth look. In fact, these two countries are fo₁
capitalizing on the changes that are reshaping Asi
of the world's shifting industrial base. As these eco
tinue to grow, other Asian manufacturing countrie₅
their lead. Anyone who has visited Malaysia o₁
knows that they are growing so fast that tracking a
their growth is like trying to hit a moving target
however, certain characteristics that have taken de
can be followed closely and observed easily.

Though it is difficult to provide hard evidence,
tries seem to have an innocence and optimism that h
seen in Europe since 1870 and the United State₅

role in society, as they do in most of Asia, and these character-istics put strict limitations on certain behavior. In Singapore and Malaysia, a person who treats other people and property with respect earns courtesy and respect in return. Behaving otherwise results in punishment that is swift, sure, and strict. Caning and prison sentences are the norm for what would be regarded as "minor infractions" in the United States; even petty thievery warrants more than a year in prison. As a delin-quent American teenager painfully learned two years ago, Singapore publicly humiliates those who destroy the property of others. Family values are not just election-time slogans in these countries, they are important building blocks of the cul-ture. Family ties are strong in Singapore and Malaysia, and they help keep the people's interests united. Because countries like Singapore and Malaysia have so little crime, they can afford to invest so much more in bettering the lives of all their citizens. Among their priorities lies building a more productive economy.

Singapore Claims Independence and Prospers

Singapore, the island at the Malay peninsula's southern tip, was part of Malaysia until 1966, when it became an indepen-dent city-state. Since claiming its independence, Singapore has proven to be one of the strongest economies in the world. A large part of its stability can probably be credited to the fact that most Singaporeans are Chinese descendants and still oper-ate with the Chinese work ethic ingrained in their minds. Unlike many other free-market countries, Singapore tradition thrives on the notion that democracy must be earned through hard work, not given freely. Because of this belief, Singapore-ans have always strived to deserve the privilege of living in a democratic society and they have protected their interests by nurturing a culture in which respect for others is paramount. Because the crime rate in Singapore is virtually nonexistent, energy that would otherwise be wasted trying to deter crimi-nals is used productively to strengthen the performance of the economy for the benefit of all Singaporeans.

Given the fact that Singapore has no natural resources of note, except its people, the prosperity of its economy in the past 30 years is astonishing. Few currencies have risen as consistently against the U.S. dollar—year after year after year—as the Singapore dollar. The stocks denominated in Singapore's currency have gone from strong to stronger. The impressive growth rates of Singapore's economy stem from two significant facts. First, Singapore has very little debt, and second, the central bank does not increase the money supply and therefore controls inflation. As a result, Singapore operates from a very stable, profit-oriented bottom line. Also, Singapore maintains a complete balance of trade with its export of manufactured products and its offering of financial services. The ultimate key to Singapore's success is consistency as is illustrated by the Singapore market index, the Straits Times, which, like the currency, falls little during bear markets and rises well in bull markets.

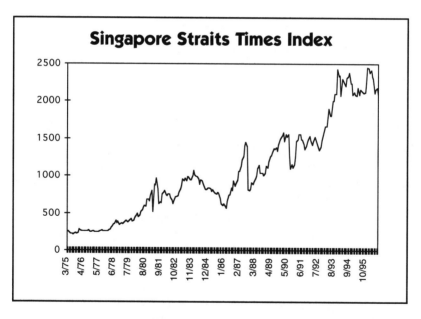

Conventional wisdom holds that if the value of a country's currency is too high, its exports will suffer and its imports will surge, causing trade deficits and a stagnant economy. Actually, the economy ended 1996 with 7 percent growth, the Singapore dollar has since risen even higher, and exports are still pouring out of the city-state. So much for conventional wisdom.

Pessimists have predicted for years that Singapore's growth would end and they were almost right in 1992 when the economy grew by "only" 5.2 percent. Since then, Singapore has been working smarter, and the exporting of high-technology manufactured goods remains its competitive mainstay. The world's two largest makers of computer sound cards, which enhance the audio-visual capacity of computers, are Singaporean and 40 percent of the world market in hard disk drives are shipped from Singapore, even though much of the assembly is done in Malaysia, where labor costs are sometimes 50 percent lower.

Success Adds Value to Exports

Singapore's success in adding more value to its exports has been the result of a planned strategic policy that the powers in charge have been able to put into action. Essentially, they intend to broaden their industrial base in order to compete with high-value, high-tech product manufacturers such as those in Japan and the United States. The government plans are easily implemented with the presence of such an able workforce as is found in Singapore; and, once again, the Chinese work ethic prevails.

An old Chinese proverb says that wealth seldom survives three generations. The first generation, born poor, works hard to build the wealth. The second generation doesn't have quite the same "fire in the belly" but nonetheless manages to maintain what the previous generation has achieved. By the third generation, however, ties to the days of struggle are weak, and the good life beckons.

Singapore's third generation is now entering the workforce. Efforts to instill in them the values that put Singapore on the map are evident everywhere, and they seem to be having a significant effect. Young people appear to be just as hard-working as their parents and grandparents. The Singaporean Chinese may thus disprove the old Chinese proverb; after all, they have proven other conventional wisdom wrong in many areas. The future there looks strong.

Profit in Its Ports

One way to profit from Singapore's future growth involves the high-tech exports being shipped out of its ports. "Shipped" is the operative word here. With its central location, Singapore is a hub for shipping between Europe and Asia, and Singapore itself does considerable inter-Asian shipping. There is so much trade there that pages and pages in the daily newspapers of Singapore and Malaysia are filled with names of ships in port. Not only is Singapore independently one of the main trading ports in the world, but ships going to and from other places use its ports as well. With all this traffic, the likelihood that ships will need repair has opened another market for Singaporean business: ship repair.

Singapore has, in fact, dominated the world's ship repair industry for almost 20 years. It has an unbeatable mixture of strategic location, sophisticated infrastructure, and competitive costs. No other maritime country can match this combination. Out of the nearly 100,000 ships that call at Singapore each year, about 3,000 stop there for repair. With an average cost per ship reaching US$650,000, this industry generates around $2 billion per year. Interestingly enough, tanker repairs account for nearly two-thirds of the total revenue because these oil-toting vessels must adhere to strict environmental guidelines and must always be "shipshape."

Almost every drop of oil being shipped from the Middle East to the booming Asian Pacific passes through Singapore. One-quarter of world tanker traffic goes from the oil producers through Singapore to Japan and Korea. If China is successful in finding oil, Singapore's position as the maritime hub to the Asian Pacific will ensure that oil tanker traffic remains and that the shipping business will grow right along with the region's economies.

Already Singapore is a regional oil grading center and the world's third largest oil refiner, yet another prime source of domestic revenue. In the most recent year, Singapore imported 66 million tons of oil, of which 40 million tons were reexported, usually at a good profit, after being refined. This is impressive for a little country with no domestic oil that imports two-thirds as much oil as South Korea but of that, manages to export an amount equal to the entire output of the oil-rich Red Sea area.

It is also an example, as in the computer industry, of how Singapore adds value to the resources that come through it and thereby produces profitable exports.

Even though the Singapore dollar has been rising, a trend that is likely to continue, the profitability of Singapore's shipyards should not be affected. In fact, they are likely to remain the world's premier ship repair yards. Unlike other repair yards, Singapore is also a huge trading port; essentially, it is like a convenience shop for tankers. Shippers save a lot of money by stopping for repairs and business simultaneously. On top of that are other savings that come from good backup services: finance and insurance facilities, modern telecommunications, efficient customs and government, and a great airport and airline (Singapore Air) that can quickly transport new crews or special equipment to the ships.

Jurong Shipyard

Jurong is a Singaporean port district that harbors Jurong Shipyard (JSL), potentially the best play among ship repair companies. Jurong is probably the best managed and most internally stable shipyard in Singapore. Productivity per employee is far above that of its competitors. JSL's management team is Chinese and maintains traditional Singaporean work ethics. The long lasting implementation of Japanese management techniques, those that stress teamwork over individualism, has paid off for this well-oiled machine. Also, more than 50 percent of all Jurong's clients are repeat customers, which reflects well on its service and management. In addition, employee relations are healthy and employee turnover is low, with the average employee having been with the company for 12 years. Deriving the majority of its revenues from ship repair, Jurong is the purest play in Singapore. It is also a company on the move.

Jurong Shipyard was founded in 1963 as a joint venture between the Singaporean government and the Japanese heavy industry conglomerate IHI. Over time, IHI's investment in JSL has dropped from 51 to 9 percent, but the connection has long served to bring in considerable Japanese business. Because the yen has appreciated even more than the Singapore dollar over the recent past and continues to do so, costs have remained stable for Japanese clients; however, the sharp slowdown in Japanese economic growth has had a similar effect on JSL's profits. While most companies with a large Japanese clientele lost money due to their recession, Jurong has remained profitable. Although JSL is presently only the third largest repair yard in Singapore, a proposed merger with the ship repair company Sembawang Corp. would make Jurong the largest ship repair company in Singapore, acccounting for 1.710 million dead-weight tons of dry dock capacity, or about half of the total docking capacity of the four largest yards in Singapore.

Jurong is also expanding overseas, another factor that has helped it weather a recent slowdown in shipping. In Iran, Jurong holds a 26 percent stake in a venture involving the shipyard Sadra Jurong. JSL will manage the shipyard for ten years, a fact that thrills ship owners because it introduces the presence of a world-class shipyard in a country rich in vital oil exports but lacking in efficient infrastructure. In China, Sembawang Jurong Corrosion, another of JSL's branches, provides tank coating and marine corrosion resistance services and is likely to become that country's most efficient ship-maintenance company. Jurong is currently looking for opportunities in Vietnam, a country with a long coastline and an equally long tradition of sea trade that for decades has languished and is only now reawakening.

Other recent developments in JSL's expansion include the 1994 acquisition of 35 percent (50 percent option) of Atlantis Construction, which has a small dock in Tuas (Jurong). Also, in April 1994, JSL set up a joint-venture company called Orient Clavon with NOL and Clavon Engineering. The company provides blasting services and already has a contract for the expansion of the Changi Airport. Finally, in January 1995, JSL contracted a project that will convert a tanker into a floating production storage and off-loading facility for Amoco Orient Petroleum Company. In addition to ship repair, Jurong now has the ability to provide services such as shipbuilding, converting, shipowning, and waste recycling and it continues to expand its home base as business demands. This all-weather shipping business provides great opportunity to profit in the booming Singaporean economy.

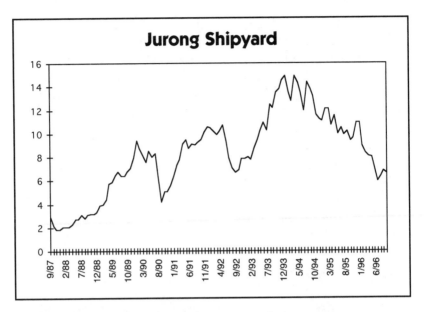

Malaysia's Ethnic Mix an Advantage

The situation in Malaysia is more complicated than that of Singapore, where the Chinese leadership virtually guarantees success. In Malaysia, the political and educational sectors are run by the Muslims (ethnic Malays); business is run by the Chinese, as it is in most Asian countries; and Indians preside over the legal, accounting, and civil service professions. This broad ethnic mix gives Malaysia distinct advantages because the greatest assets of each culture work together in the mainstream.

Although Malaysia holds within it an ethnic crossroads of the three largest countries in Asia—China, India, and Indonesia—it hasn't had serious ethnic strife for years. The Malay Muslims have, however, instituted an affirmative action program that, through quotas, gives the Muslims an edge over the Chinese in certain areas of society. More and more, the unproductive effects of this program are becoming evident, so it may not last. As with the affirmative action program in the United States, the creation of a "level playing field" has become a natural deterrent to productivity and is being reconsidered.

Naturally, there are tensions and some resentment of the economically successful, as there are in any country. One program that is having a positive effect, however, allows every

Malaysian to have a stake in the continued economic growth of the country. The poorest Malaysians are given interest-free loans to enable them to invest in special unit trusts that, in turn, invest in a broad group of stocks, bonds, and government securities. Through this program, Malaysians are given hope and motivation rather than constant negation. They are then more willing to participate in the social and economic security, growth, and stability of their country.

Malaysia, Singapore's northern neighbor, has the potential to grow in percentage terms even more than Singapore. Wages are lower in Malaysia, it has much more land and a greater population. Manufacturing is booming in Malaysia, and as an investment play, certain companies prove to be a safe bet.

Sime Darby

Sime Darby is perhaps the bluest chip in the land. Founded nearly a century ago and with a current market capitalization of nearly US$4 billion, it has recently performed more like a lucky penny stock. From January 1995 to January 1997, Sime Darby's stock price has climbed from US$3.37 to US$7.03, a two-year return of 208 percent. Despite this solid growth, Sime Darby is known in Malaysia as a very conservative company. Unlike the better known companies, Sime Darby does not promote itself. It simply goes about business as usual and consequently generates astounding results. Not surprisingly, among fund managers and institutions that invest in Malaysia, this $4 billion company is very well known.

It used to be easy to describe Sime Darby as a proxy for the nonfinancial sectors of the Malaysian economy, meaning agriculture and manufacturing. Malaysian agricultural interests are being downplayed now due to cheaper labor costs in neighboring Indonesia. The production of palm oil and rubber remains strong domestically, and Sime Darby continues to play a big role in the industry. More important for the future are Sime Darby's manufacturing-related enterprises, not just in Malaysia but in other key parts of Asia.

Sime Darby has had the Caterpillar tractor franchise for part of Malaysia since the 1920s. Today, it has the franchise for all of Malaysia, Singapore, Hong Kong, Brunei, and, most excitingly, the three coastal provinces of China, an area of extremely high growth. Australia's Queensland; Papua, New Guinea; and the Solomon Islands are included in the franchises as well.

In terms of basic construction, Sime Darby is very well placed to continue to profit from the economic rise of Asia. Its tractor business ensures an interest in new infrastructure and real development, but when all is said and done, Sime Darby stands to profit even further. As groups of industrialists and entrepreneurs mushroom into existence creating a nouveau riche sector, they will buy the same high-priced status items as those of "Yuppies" in the West. Anticipating this, Sime Darby has acquired the BMW franchise for Hong Kong and the coastal Chinese provinces. The company has also acquired the Ford and Mitsubishi franchises for Hong Kong (which will inevitably service the same coastal provinces) and the Land Rover franchise for Malaysia. We have seen the "status symbol" car trend in the United States, Japan, Germany, and many other countries; there is no reason to believe that Asia won't show off too!

Not nearly as glamorous, but extremely important, are two Sime Darby factories that have capitalized on the manufacturing shift and are located in China. One makes low-cost/high-quality

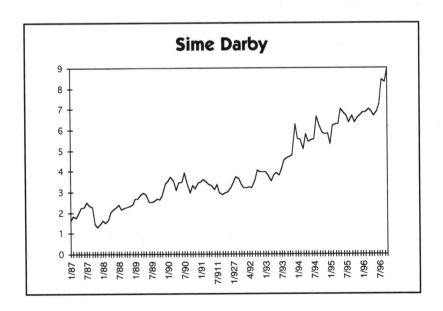

cardboard boxes for packaging and shipping Asian electronic goods that continue to flood the world's markets. The other makes low-cost rubber footwear that can potentially protect the millions of cold, water-logged feet that work in the agricultural fields all over Asia. Both successfully service a needy niche market and have potential to become hugely profitable.

Being a conglomerate, Sime Darby has properties world-wide. It operates more than 200 businesses in some of the most rapidly growing economies in the world. Using Malaysia as its base, the company has expanded into attractive regions and is firmly positioned to profit from Southeast Asia's increasing importance. For both the short and long term, Sime Darby comes highly recommended based on its blue chip status, its stability, and its earning potential from diverse operations throughout the high growth economies of the Asia-Pacific region.

Nylex

Several other companies are poised to profit from the construction and manufacturing boom in Malaysia. Those companies that have a foot in the door are the ones who can inexpensively produce materials needed in heavy industry. For

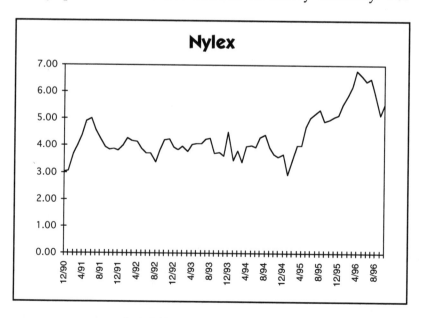

instance, the Malaysian company, Nylex (Malaysia) Berhad has an engineering division that designs, manufactures, supplies, installs, and maintains electric power switch gear and distribution systems. Another division of the same company makes and markets vinyl-coated fabrics and plastic packaging. A third makes and markets building products, particularly metal roofing tiles and glass-wool insulation. Yet another division makes and sells glass containers for which demand outweighs current full-time production. Nylex, like many Singaporean companies, is interested in higher-value-added manufacturing that cuts costs and increases revenues by providing parts and labor within the same company. Nylex, which has been in existence just since 1990, is a subsidiary of the British blue chip BTR plc. Its immediate parent is BTR Nylex Ltd. of Australia through which its activities might extend into China. Currently, all forecasts point upward; it is a good buy.

Clipsal

Clipsal Industries in Singapore develops, manufactures, and markets high-quality electrical installation products for the building trade: electrical wiring accessories, circuit breakers,

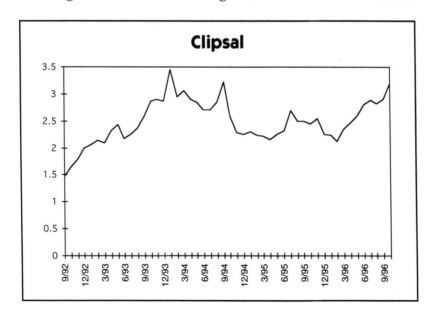

and switches. The Clipsal brands are well known for quality in the building industry, with market shares estimated at 60 percent in Hong Kong, 40 to 45 percent in Singapore and Malaysia, 60 percent in Australia where it also has a 50 percent stake in Gerard Industries' extensive electrical product line, and 90 percent of the high-end market in China. Additionally, Clipsal is making strong inroads in Taiwan, Vietnam, South Africa, the Middle East, and India. Right in line with its strategy for growth, Clipsal is setting up factories in those regions that are sure to boom.

Leader Universal Holdings

In Malaysia, Leader Universal Holdings (LUH) manufactures and sells electrical and household wires, telecommunication and power cables, aluminum rods, and household and fiber-optic cables. Where Clipsal mainly sells to private construction companies, LUH's sales are primarily to the Malaysian utilities Tenaga and Telekom, whose robust demand for cable had sent profits through the roof between 1993 and 1995. However, in 1996 earnings have been flat and, since September 1994, LUH's stock price has been cut in half. But being the Malaysian market forerunner in power and

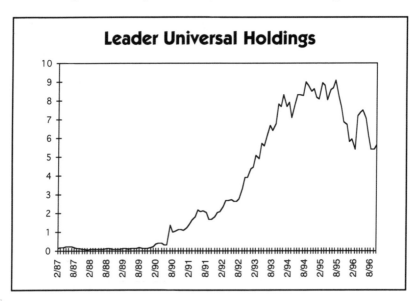

telecommunications, it should continue to benefit from heavy increases in infrastructure spending (budgeted at 22 billion ringgit over the next five years) and may be a good opportunity at these prices.

Kian Joo Can Factory

A Malaysian manufacturer that is also a play on consumer spending is Kian Joo Can Factory Berhad. Its products include tin cans, two-piece aluminum cans, polyethylene (PET) products, and corrugated cardboard cartons. Kian Joo is the leading manufacturer of cans in Malaysia and with only one competitor, its growth curve looks like the ascending northern slope of Mt. Kilimanjaro. Kian Joo is positioned to expand its business in the Asia-Pacific region, especially Vietnam, and has already become involved in a joint-venture with Smorgon Consolidated Industries of Australia to produce more PET bottles.

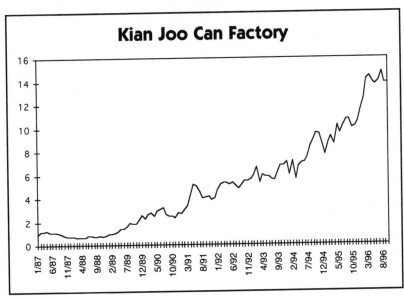

Bakrie & Brothers

P.T. Bakrie & Brothers, "Bakrie," is one of Indonesia's most dynamic listed companies. Employing 8,600, the company operates in three industries: infrastructure support, plantations, and telecommunications. The company's origins can be traced back to 1942, when established as a commodities trading company by Indonesian businessman Achmad Bakrie. While still majority-owned by the Bakrie family, and ultimately directed by the eldest son, Aburizal, the company's operations are professionally run by internationally trained managers. Since 1983 the company has concentrated on infrastructure support, including steel pipe manufacturing, steel structures, and fiber cement materials. In the '90s, the company emerged as a leader in plantations and agribusiness, and more recently, the company has entered the telecommunications industry, and invested substantially in mining.

In 1959, Bakrie started production as Indonesia's first steel pipe manufacturer, and continues to be the country's largest. Bakrie's activities include the manufacture of welded and seamless steel pipes, corrugated steel products, auto components, fiber cement-based building products, as well as civil engineering projects, mechanical plant and equipment installations. Bakrie has proven capabilities in designing, constructing, and supervising a spectrum of infrastructure projects: bridges, power transmission towers, and irrigation systems. Bakrie's wide-ranging businesses provide vertical integration and synergies to help meet Indonesia's rapidly growing demand for infrastructure.

Plantations

This division owns 55,000 hectares (135,900 acres) of fertile land in Sumatra. Primarily rubber plantations, annual rubber extraction is approximately 22,000 tons. The company is also developing a substantial oil palm plantation. At present, the company is the world's only producer of low-protein cream latex, a high value-added product used extensively in a range of specialty applications, notably, the prevention of latex allergies.

Telecommunications

Since 1989, the company has been awarded contracts for the installation of more than 420,000 telephone lines. More than 60 percent of these lines have been granted as build-operate-transfer projects, meaning that for a period of time, telephone fees will accrue to Bakrie, after which the lines will be handed over to Telkom Indonesia. In 1994, PTT Telecom (Netherlands) purchased a 30 percent stake in Bakrie's telecom division for US$90 million, and contributing expertise and capital. Bakrie has installed 121,000 traditional fixed lines, while the next 280,000 (250,000 in Jakarta) will be using Hughes Electronics' Flexible Overlay Network (FONET) system, which uses wireless technology to cheaply and quickly emulate fixed line installations. Bakrie is also developing a low-cost Advanced Rural Telephone System in partnership with the national telecom company, PT Telkom, to provide low-cost digital telecommunications to scattered and thinly populated areas as are typical for much of Indonesia. The company also owns cellular operations in Australia, and has signed a memorandum of understanding to install phone lines in Vietnam.

Strategic Investments

In 1994, Bakrie purchased 49 percent of a company that owns 9.4 percent (an effective 4.7 percent stake) of PT Freeport Indonesia, a copper, gold, and silver mining company that has concession rights over the world's single largest gold reserve and the third largest open pit copper reserve. Proven and probable reserves are more than 28 billion pounds of copper, 40 million ounces of gold, and 81 million ounces of silver. Wholly owned subsidiary Bakrie Power Corp has a 20 percent interest in a project to build a 200-megawatt power plant in Lampung, a 30 percent stake in a project to build a 1,200 MW power plant in Tanjung Jati, and a 25 percent stake in a project to build a 400 MW power plant in Serpong. Bakrie also is involved in a joint venture with Mitsubishi Kasei to manufacture P.T.A., used in synthetic fibers, plastics, and resins.

Long-Term Strategy

Bakrie has stated that its long-term strategy is to become an undisputed leader in Indonesian Telecommunications, just as they are recognized leaders in infrastructure support and plantation industries. The company considers the infrastructure and telecommunications industries as the backbone of the fast-growing Indonesian economy. Taking advantage of Indonesia's surging direct foreign investment, Bakrie is constantly seeking out foreign joint-venture partners to add technical expertise and financing for new projects.

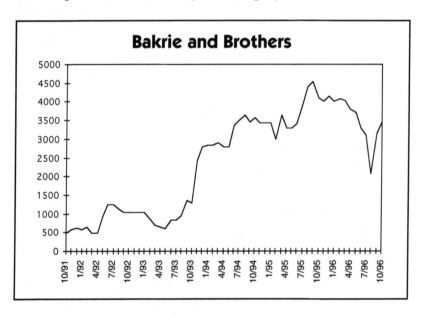

New World Development

New World Development is one of the largest integrated property, construction, and hotel groups in Hong Kong, which is also aggressively pursuing opportunities in Chinese land development, infrastructure projects, and hotel management. The backbone of New World's operating profit comes from property development in Hong Kong, which is characterized by its low land bank cost, large gross floor area under construction, and substantial farmland reserves. Its current land bank reserves amount to 17 million square feet.

New World's projects stand to benefit from the decentralization of Hong Kong's residential projects, driven in the long run by increased demand for lower cost housing by Chinese immigrants. The company won the contract for the redevelopment of the Headquarters of the Mass Transit Railway Corporation in Kowloon Bay. The proximity of some of New

World's land bank to the headquarters should make projects in this area more valuable for future development.

Property investment (for rental income) is showing steady growth, with capacity expansion coming in the next three years as certain office and retail properties are completed. The group's policy is to look for new property investment opportunities in the territory, as it provides stable, recurrent income flows. New World is one of the top ten landlords in Hong Kong, retaining a portfolio of 8.2 million square feet.

New World also has a large presence in the hotel industry: it owns five high-priced hotels in Hong Kong, with rates averaging from US$100/night to US$300/night. The firm owns 64 percent of New World Hotels International, owning or managing over a dozen hotels primarily in Hong Kong and China, with further hotels under development in Asia. The Renaissance Hotel Group was spun off and listed in the United States, but New World indirectly retains a 37.7 percent interest through New World Hotels. Renaissance Hotel Group manages more than 130 hotels around the world under the Renaissance, New World, and Ramada brand names.

New World is one of the most aggressive players in China investments, comprising more than an estimated US$1.4 billion, primarily in lower-risk infrastructure projects and high return property developments. In infrastructure, their projects include three power plants, a water plant, seven highway and bridge projects, an airport, and ten industrial projects. In property development, New World's early investments in China property have produced low land costs—and most of their land is in Beijing, Shanghai, and Guangzhou, where prices have escalated since 1991. The existing land bank should be sufficient for development over the next two decades. Much of New World's China property development land bank is directed toward the Low Cost Housing Scheme, whereby local governments guarantee after-tax returns on investment. New World sees China as a long-term commitment, with profits expected to become significant only in 1997 and beyond. It is possible that New World may follow the current trend of spinning off and separately listing a China holding company directed toward Chinese property development.

In October 1995, New World successfully spun off and listed New World Infrastructure, now 69 percent owned by New World, raising HK$2.1 billion. NWI will run the company's existing container terminal and tunnel operations in Hong Kong as well as its highway projects, power stations, airport, and bridge in China.

New World's strategy shall retain its focus on property development, property investment, and infrastructure projects in Hong Kong and People's Republic of China, with China limited to 20 to 25 percent of assets. Hotel businesses will be expanded worldwide, and the company's goal is to derive half of its operating profits from recurrent sources (nonproperty development) in the long run. This year, New World began a big push into Hong Kong telecommunications, as it and its partners will be investing HK$1 billion to offer local and international telephone, paging, and data and multimedia communication services.

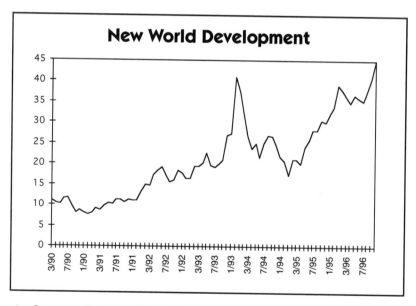

A Snapshot of the Future

In the ever-changing region of Southeast Asia, you can be sure that companies will continue to emerge. The few that are listed provide only a snapshot of what is to come, but they certainly provide an excellent starting block and an opportunity for profit over the next decade.

12

Pre-Emerging Economies: Hunting for Investments in the Last Developing Frontiers

The Pre-Emerging Markets Trend

A very distinctive economic development pattern directs the building blocks that form modern nations. Before an economy becomes emergent, and certainly before it is industrialized or modern, it passes through the most crucial stage in its development: the pre-emerging market phase.

Marked by a lack of infrastructure both financially and technologically, countries of pre-emerging status typically struggle to break the barriers that prevent them from growing. One necessary step in development is the formation of a stock exchange without which sophisticated investments cannot be made. Usually, these financial establishments lack liquidity and list few companies since most remain private. However, they represent the beginning of economic growth and can be very profitable.

Another step is the improvement of infrastructure, such as telephone lines, roads, and electric and hydroelectric power, which are necessary for the exchange and transport of goods and information that enable the country to prosper. One of the more difficult transitions to make is the shift from the old ways of management to competitive, modern methods. Frequently, growth of pre-emerging public companies is thwarted because of a lack of technology, inefficiency, and a day-to-day mentality that limits the ability to project and proceed with growth. Once the criteria for development is met, these pre-emerging countries often blossom into productive emerging market economies.

Africa, the Last Investment Frontier

Every continent but Africa has recently enjoyed spectacular investment returns. In fact, the inhabitants of most African countries are poorer today than they were a generation ago. The combined gross domestic product of all the African countries (except South Africa) is smaller than that of Belgium. Some of these nations do not even have a money economy. In Zambia, for example, only 500,000 of its 9 million people have formal jobs with wages. Many live at a subsistence level, as they have for thousands of years. Now, the collapse of communism and the spread of free market capitalism have introduced ideas to many of these nations and are tempting many countries to develop "westernized" economies.

Not surprisingly, Africa is the last great investment frontier. Investment assets there are the world's cheapest. Only one major stock exchange, in Johannesburg, South Africa, exists on the entire continent, and it has become a venue for mixing Western capital with the few African companies large enough to be listed.

There are also stock markets in other African countries, and new ones continue to open. Recently, a dozen were operating in countries such as Morocco, Zimbabwe, Kenya, Tunisia, and Nigeria. Combined, they have a total market capitalization of just 6 percent of the South African exchange, which is comparable to that of the Mexican Bolsa.

Even though the African market is small, there are two reasons to look more closely at it. First, it has by far the world's cheapest stock markets. Companies trade at a mere three or four times annual earnings, compared with 50 or 60 times earnings on the "hot" stocks of markets in more industrialized countries. Second, many African governments are pursuing sensible economic policies which, for the first time, open the doors for investment and growth.

Fifty-two countries share the African continent. Although these countries differ in many ways, several are clearly moving toward a modern standard of living. The individual circumstances of these countries may differ, but they have one thing in common: After years of Soviet-style socialism, all have become almost flamboyantly free-market oriented.

Zimbabwe, a Country with Optimism

Zimbabwe, which began to emerge from self-imposed isolation in the late 1980s, has no exchange controls or import controls, and anyone with as little as $500 can open a bank account in the currency of his or her choice, something that cannot be done in the United States. This situation is extraordinary given that until recently the government of Robert Mugabe was committed to socialism, and it is Mugabe who now presides over newly reformed policies that now encourage Zimbabwe to be productive and competitive. Compared to all other African nations except South Africa, Zimbabwe's infrastructure is excellent. Roads, hotels, and telecommunications are surprisingly good. Of particular interest to investors is its stock market, which is the third largest in Africa (after South Africa and Morocco). There are 52 companies on Zimbabwe's industrial exchange, and 6 on its mining exchange. As of early 1995, the total market capitalization was about $2 billion.

The optimism that propels the country's people in general is reflected on the floor of the Zimbabwe Stock Exchange (ZSE) whose general index increased 50 percent during the first half of 1994. And, more importantly, the stock exchange authorities are trying to expand the number of shareholders to include most Zimbabweans. According to Mark Tumner, the ZSE chairman, they are even conducting a public awareness campaign that reaches down to the level of senior schools, sometimes to kids as young as 13, and encourages interest and participation in the expansion of the economy. The ZSE has been open for foreign investment since June 1993, but because it is still in the pre-emerging stage, most of the established companies also list themselves on the South African market next door.

As countries like Zimbabwe grow, their demand for energy and energy sources will inevitably increase, too. Other than renewable sources of energy, such as solar and wind power, natural gas is the cleanest choice for energy, but unfortunately, there is not enough to meet demands. Coal is the only viable alternative at this stage of development since it is a natural resource in many African countries.

Long derided and undervalued, coal may be making a comeback for two reasons. First, the hazards of nuclear power are becoming more evident. Older power plants are showing a level of structural stress beyond our worst forecasts and it is often much less costly to build a new nuclear power plant than to fix an old one. Also, nuclear power plants are very unpopular among potential neighbors because of the health and safety hazards they represent. Another reason for the comeback of coal is that new technologies have made it cleaner. Chemicals applied after mining can now break down the coal, removing much of the fossil, improving the grade, and refining it until it is almost free of toxins and much more desirable for use.

Wankie Colliery

African companies like Wankie Colliery of Zimbabwe stand to benefit from the advances in the coal refining industry. Wankie's coal production satisfies Zimbabwe's needs and more. The share price has risen from $5 in September 1993 to $45 in January 1997, an increase of 900 percent.

Wankie's market capitalization is only about $46 million, and the stock price-earnings (PE) ratio a mere 8.5, when coal mines in neighboring South Africa trade at PE ratios of 15. Part of the reason for Wankie's low PE ratio is that shipping the company's coal from Zimbabwe to the nearest seaport in Mozambique, a country still struggling to achieve even pre-emerging status, is difficult. But a more important reason concerns Wankie's ownership. The government owns a substantial chunk (40 percent) of the company and also runs it; investors simply lack confidence in state-run enterprises and are discouraged from investing because of it. As a result, the stock prices will remain low until investors gain confidence in the operation or until the government lets go of its share.

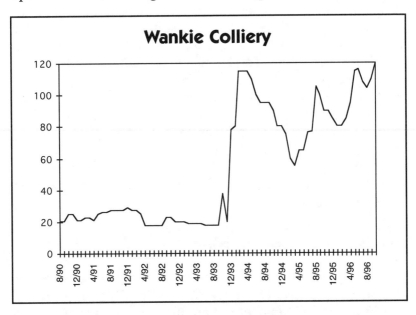

There is no guarantee that the Zimbabwean government will not run Wankie into the ground due to poor management, a fate that crippled many coal mines in Eastern Europe. If the government concedes its control and allows this mine to be privatized, Wankie Colliery stock may soar. Unfortunately, we must wait to see what happens. Even so, Wankie's stock is cheap and as Zimbabwe grows and needs more power, and as it becomes easier to transport and export the coal, the price should eventually rise.

Namibia, Newly Independent and Growing

Namibia is a newly independent country in southwest Africa. Larger than twice the size of France, it has a population of only 1.4 million people. First a German colony, then a protectorate of South Africa, Namibia has been on its own since

1990. Economic growth is sailing along at 3 percent per year and per-capita income is equal to US$1,400 per year, which is quite high for Africa.

The country's infrastructure is very good. There are about 9,000 miles of paved roads, 1,500 miles of railroad, and good telephone service. In the financial realm, the Namibian dollar is tied to the South African rand. Most of the major international firms are there. The Namibian system welcomes a free market economy and even allows profits to be taken out of the country. It provides a very capitalist-friendly atmosphere for investment. Company taxation levels have been reduced during each of the past two years, and there is no capital gains tax on any profits made by investing on the new Namibia stock exchange. Presently, only five companies are listed, but the brokerage and trading fees and commissions could be the most competitive in Africa.

Ocean Diamond Mining

One of the five companies listed on Namibia's stock exchange is Ocean Diamond Mining (ODM), a company poised to take advantage of Namibia's natural resources. As yet, vast areas of the country have not been fully explored for its resource development potential. But one thing is certain: Some of the world's richest diamond mines are in Namibia.

The Orange River designates the southern border of Namibia and has served as a transport route for billions of carats of diamonds from the rich South African diamond pipes. As the inland pipes eroded over millions of years, diamonds were carried along the Orange River and deposited in the sea along Namibia's coastline. Many became embedded in land along the coast as well. It has been estimated that for every carat in the inland diamond pipes, 15 eroded along the Orange River.

DeBeers, the giant South African diamond cartel, holds vast coastal and offshore territories under license, and has held them since the Germans left in 1918. Over the years, DeBeers has pulled diamonds valued at $33 billion in today's dollars. The newly independent Namibia, however, is forcing DeBeers to give up some of its holdings both on and offshore and to put them up for bid, thus opening the door for smaller diamond miners to come in.

Ocean Diamond Mining had a second boat come on line in 1996 and pulled an average of 180 carats of diamonds from the sea bed per day through the first half of 1996, giving this small company a $1.43 million profit, a 333 percent increase over the first six months of 1995. A third boat will boost profits well into the millions. Already ODM's stock has risen from $.01 in 1991 to $3 in 1997. The company is valued at 40 times earnings. Although it may not now be the wisest investment, if productivity increases and management develops, that situation may change. (ODM's stock also trades on the larger South African exchange.)

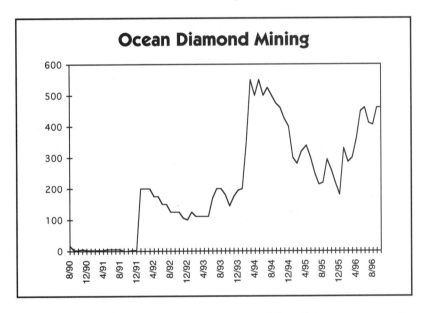

Presently, the investment options in Namibia are extremely limited. But this country continues to encourage free-marke-teers and investment and should develop nicely in the next decade.

Tanzania, Two Investment Advantages

Tanzania is rare among African countries for having done away with the bane of that continent: tribalism. Other countries have reached accommodations in this regard; for example,

Zimbabwe's two major tribes now share power after years of civil war. But Tanzanians simply do not feel the pull of any tribe. In light of the situation in neighboring Rwanda, this is a tremendous advantage.

Tanzania's other advantage has to do with its government's outlook. After achieving independence from Britain, Tanzania was ruled by Julius Nyerere, whose Soviet-based economic model brought rigid state control and virtually abolished private enterprise. But after 25 years, Nyerere recognized that his policy was not serving the nation, and he resigned.

Tanzania's government has since become very free-market-oriented. Since 1992, incentives have been put in place to lure investors into putting capital into old and new businesses in Tanzania. Among the incentives extended to investors is a five-year tax holiday, during which they are not taxed on dividends and interest, capital gains, or imports. In addition, generous allowances are given for the wear and tear on buildings and equipment and investors are free to have accounts in any foreign currency they desire.

These investment advantages aren't enough to launch Tanzania into a competitive market environment. Typical of a pre-emerging economy its roads are in dreadful shape, its railways are decomposed, and telecommunications and power supplies are spotty. Until the government realizes the importance of infrastructure to the country's development, it will impede economic progress. These obstacles make it uncertain whether Tanzania will soon reach the emerging economy stage. If it does reach this stage, investors stand to make a lot of money.

Zambia, Undiscovered Investment Opportunity

Zambia is another African country that merits attention but as yet remains fairly undiscovered by investors. As a British colony, Zambia was known as Northern Rhodesia, and like many other African countries, Zambia tried full socialism after independence in the early 1960s. Now, like Tanzania, Zambia's laws lean toward free-market solutions. Unlike Tanzania, however, Zambia's roads and telecommunications infrastructure are excellent, and may help provide the leg up the country needs to achieve emerging market status.

One possible disadvantage that may hamper Zambia's development is its lack of diversity. The economy is presently tied too much to metals mining; its stock exchange is not diversified out of the metals sector and is not very liquid. Zambia is the world's largest producer of cobalt, a "strategic metal" vital to jet engines and other high-technology machinery. It is also a big world supplier of copper. This reliance on metals won't be a disadvantage if commodity prices rise, but if they fall, the country's economy could be hurt badly.

If inflation becomes a problem, the minerals produced by Zambian mines will become more valuable. Even so, the government, which nationalized the big copper mines 30 years ago, has done a poor job of running them and consequently the outputs have decreased each year. If the government gets out of the mining business, and if it continues its first tentative steps toward capitalism, Zambia will be an up-and-coming economy. The signs are encouraging. In the past three years, there has been a huge increase in the number of small-scale individual enterprises operating in Zambia. Although much of this entrepreneurship is on the "pushcart" level, it should be taken seriously since many companies, such as McDonald's Corporation, Nathan's Famous Inc., Ben and Jerry's, and Mrs. Fields to name a few, have sprung from pushcart peddlers all over the United States.

Funds Specializing in Pre-Emerging African Nations

Investors who don't want to limit themselves to one African country or stock but do want to invest in pre-emerging economies can look forward to an increasing number of funds specializing in this region. Already Morgan Stanley's African Investment Fund, Alliance Capital's Southern African Fund, and Robert Flemings' United Kingdom-based New South

Africa Fund and others have been created. Although these funds focus mainly on companies of the South African stock exchange, they will be the first to dive into other opportunities as they develop. For now, it is unclear how much good quality stock investors will have to choose from in pre-emerging African nations.

Companies in Pre-Emerging Economies in Eastern Europe

Finding many good quality companies to invest in is a problem in all pre-emerging economies. The Czech Republic is an example of a country struggling to break into the world's competitive economic market, but it is still in the very formative stages of development. Although the Czech transition has been one of the least painful and more advanced of the Eastern European nations, and although its economy is well on the way to emerging status, there are simply not enough good companies in which to invest.

Five years ago, when the "velvet revolution" occurred, 2 percent of the country's assets were in private hands; now, the figure is rapidly approaching 80 percent. The state's budget is balanced, inflation is relatively moderate, and unemployment is just over 3 percent. Much of this progress can be attributed to Prime Minister Vaclav Klaus's firm pro-market reform policy.

Overall, the Czech Republic is "emerging" into the developed world, and the country is the only former communist state to win an investment-grade rating from Moody's and Standard & Poor's. Even so, surprisingly few investment-grade companies exist. The only way to easily participate in the growth of the Czech Republic is to buy into a fund. The Czech Republic Fund is listed on the New York Stock Exchange, but even this is only 65 percent invested in Czech assets. The rest goes for companies in Austria, Hungary, Poland, and Slovakia.

Unfortunately, Slovakia has shown us what can go wrong in Eastern Europe, and indeed, in any pre-emerging economy. Many people in Slovakia are deeply suspicious of privatization

End vs. Closed-End Funds

are two primary differences between open-end and
d funds. Open-end funds stand ready to issue new
redeem outstanding shares on a continuous basis and
heir "net asset value." With an open-end fund, the
ney that is invested, the larger the fund grows.
d funds have a fixed number of shares outstanding
e at a market price determined by supply and
Shares often trade at a discount to their net asset
may trade at a premium if the fund is particularly
vith investors. Most funds that invest in a single
e closed-end funds.

nd No-Load Funds

oortant distinction to keep in mind when purchasing
whether or not the fund has a sales charge or *load*.
nds marketed through brokerage firms are typically
. There are two types of loads: Front-end, paid at the
rchase, and back-end, paid at the time of redemp-
-load fund is purchased directly from the mutual
oany and has no sales charge. No-load funds may,
harge fees to cover the costs associated with mar-
operating the fund.

mily

nutual fund companies offer a variety of funds, each
ent goals, strategies, and risk profile. A "family" of
the investor the ability to move his or her money
o fund, within the family, in response to changing
iditions. Most fund companies also offer the
advantage of telephones transfers and automatic
investment.

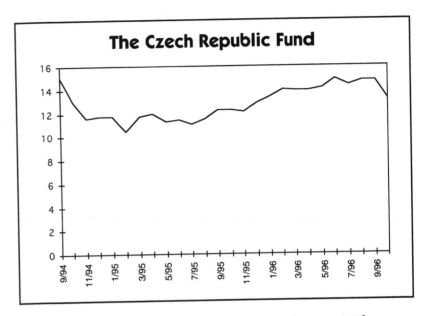

and many attempts to privatize have been thwarted. The same danger could arise in the Czech Republic, so investors should choose investments very carefully in this part of the world. Once these countries get their political and economic "acts" together, there may be some direct investments available that will be much safer than others. The worldwide trend toward free markets is unstoppable, and when these markets finally develop, they will present even more exciting investment opportunities.

13

Mutual Fun
the Most
Ways to I
Emerging

Mutual funds appear to be th
for individual investors in the
mutual funds was born out of de
person, to earn the best possible r
principal to the least amount of
such an opportunity since they a
offer greater diversification than
the average investor.

Perhaps the most important
recent mutual fund explosion is
for today's investor. There are lit
able to the investing public. The
funds as well as load and no-lo
offer the potential for growth, in
as well as funds that invest ir
countries, even the performance
the investor may choose funds tl
foreign, or global.

Open

Ther
closed-e
shares o
trade at
more n
Closed-
and tra
demand
value b
popular
country

Load

An i
a fund
Mutual
load fur
time of
tion. A
fund co
howeve
keting a

Fund

Mar
with dif
funds o
from fu
market
investor
dividen

Fund's Characteristics

There are several mutual fund characteristics that the investor should investigate prior to investing in a fund. The most important characteristic is performance, what kind of return the fund has provided over the past five to ten years. Note how the performance of the fund in question compares with funds with similar objectives. Analyze not only the size of the returns but the consistency of the returns as well. Funds that are consistently good performers are preferable to those with very high returns some years accompanied by substandard returns in other years. The investor should also look at the experience of the fund manager and the risk associated with his or her management style. The investor should try to match his or her risk tolerance and investment objective with that of the fund manager. Finally, as mentioned previously, there are often costs associated with purchasing a mutual fund, and these costs should be scrutinized to see how a fund stacks up against others in its category. Sales loads and expense ratios will determine how much of your money is actually working for you.

There are several rating services the investor can use to analyze the investment objectives, performance histories, and risk profiles of the many mutual funds offered to the investing public. Lipper Analytical Services, Inc. and Morningstar, Inc. are two of the most respected analytical services available to investors searching for the most suitable mutual fund investment.

The Unit Trust

In addition to the fund types outlined, a unique type of closed-end investment company, the Unit Trust, warrants mention in this section. The Unit Trust, as the name implies, consists of units of ownership in a fixed portfolio of securities. Usually, the portfolio is acquired before the units are offered to the public. Once the offering is complete, the portfolio remains the same throughout the life of the trust and, like the shares of a closed-end fund, the number of units of ownership is fixed.

Global Diversification

As mentioned previously, mutual funds afford the individual investor the opportunity to achieve much greater asset diversification than would be attainable if he or she had to purchase individual securities. With that goal in mind, there are a number of ways to achieve global diversification through mutual funds. In the United States, the investor may purchase open-end and closed-end funds that invest either globally or internationally. He or she may also purchase a fund that invests in a single country, known as a country fund. These are typically closed-end funds. The individual investor may also purchase closed-end funds offered on foreign exchanges. However, the Securities and Exchange Commission will not permit the U.S. investor to purchase open-end funds offered in foreign countries as they are not registered to do business in this country.

Investing in Emerging Global Trends

There are a variety of funds available that provide the opportunity to invest in emerging global trends. While there are hundreds of relatively new funds that hope to capitalize on the popularity of everything from air transportation to utilities, this section will focus on only those funds that are offered by established mutual fund companies with long-term track records.

Investing in Companies That Are Teaching Our Kids

Technology is reshaping the education field like never before. Advances in computer software and multimedia technology have not only made learning more exciting and enjoyable for the students but are also the keys to returning our nation's educational system to the forefront.

The Fidelity Selects family of mutual funds offer mutual funds that focus on individual industries. They offer both a Fidelity Select Multimedia Fund and a Fidelity Select Software and Computer Fund. Fidelity is the biggest name in mutual funds and has an excellent reputation in the industry. They also lay claim to having the world's largest fund, the Fidelity Magellon Fund with more than $55 billion in assets. Fidelity offers families of both load and no-load funds. The select funds have both a front and a back-end load totaling approximately 3.75 percent. The Multimedia Fund carries Morningstar's highest five-star rating while the Software and Computer Fund has a four-star rating. They have five/ten-year total annualized returns of 25.02/17.34 percent and 27.75/17.96 percent, respectively. These funds are highlighted because they invest exclusively in those industries most likely to benefit from the education trend. However, an investor may gain exposure to those industries through a variety of other funds that have at least a portion of their holdings represented in those sectors.

The Entertainment Boom

As is the case with education, computer technology is revolutionizing the entertainment industry. Advances in computer graphics has changed the way Hollywood creates motion pictures. Digital technology is in the process of allowing manufacturers to combine a variety of separate media into one. Interactive television will become a reality in the not-so-distant future. Finally, fiber optics has permitted the information superhighway, via the Internet, to become the fastest growing information and entertainment source in the '90s.

Companies that are at the forefront of computer and electronic technology stand to benefit most from these advances in the entertainment industry. As a result of the lessening distinction between entertainment and education, the two Fidelity Select Funds mentioned in the education section would provide exposure to companies active in the entertainment arena. Two additional open-end funds that would also provide exposure to advances in entertainment are the Alliance Technology Fund and the Fidelity Select Electronics Fund. The Alliance Technology Fund has a 4.25 percent front-end load, while the Fidelity Select Electronics fund has both a front and back-end load totaling 3.75 percent. The Alliance fund has a Morningstar rating of five stars, and the Fidelity fund carries a four-star rating. These funds have five/ten-year total annualized returns of 29.59/17.47% and 32.6/14.76 percent, respectively.

Investing on Both Sides of the Environmental Trend

There is increasing sentiment among the populace that man should no longer be permitted to destroy the environment in the name of progress and material gratification. From the industrial revolution right through the booming '80s, creating and consuming took a front seat to conservation. Now with increasing threats from such phenomena as global warming and a depleted ozone layer, governments are enacting legislation that not only forces companies to be more responsible in the future but to repair the damage resulting from the past. This relatively new environmental consciousness has created opportunity for companies that develop efficient solutions for cleaning up the environment as well as a practical means of protecting it going forward.

Companies that specialize in such areas as environmental cleanup, pollution control, and recycling should benefit most from the environmental trend. Two funds that invest almost exclusively in companies operating in these areas are the Alliance Global Environment Fund and the Fidelity Select Environmental Services Fund. Neither fund has a stellar performance track record and in fact, they carry Morningstar ratings of three stars and one star, respectively. However, they do warrant mention as they are two of the few funds that invest exclusively in the environmental sector. The Alliance Fund was created in 1990 and is a closed-end fund with a three/five-year NAV total returns of 16.29/5.36 percent.

In the latter part of 1996, the fund traded at a discount to NAV of approximately 21.5 percent. The Fidelity Environmental Services Fund was created in 1989 and, like the other Fidelity Select Funds, is open-ended. This fund has three/five-year total annualized returns of 10.89/6.01 percent.

Investing in Companies That Tackle Crime

An ever-increasing crime rate, combined with the personal insecurity that accompanies it, has laid the foundation for another relatively new and rapidly expanding industrial sector. Sadly, personal and institutional security firms have flourished during this decade like never before. Because of the relative newness of the industry, as well as the comparatively small number of firms focusing their attention in this area, there are no mutual funds devoted strictly to the crime-tackling sector. However, there are a number of funds that invest in small to mid-sized emerging growth companies, such as Wackenhut Corrections Corp. and Corrections Corp. of America. Fund literature should indicate the companies that currently comprise each fund's holdings. Be sure to choose a fund offered by a well-known mutual fund company that has a solid record of performance.

Investing in Biotechnology

Hunger and disease have plagued mankind since the beginning of time. For just about as long a period of time, man has worked to discover ways to feed an ever-expanding population and care for the world's sick. Biotechnology allows engineers and scientists to rearrange the chemical makeup of plant and animal life for the purpose of creating better and more affordable food and drugs. This is another relatively new field that offers incredible growth potential.

Once again, Fidelity offers the investor the most pure play on the biotechnology sector with the Fidelity Select Biotechnology Fund. This is an open-ended fund with a total load of 3.75 percent. It has provided five/ten-year total annualized returns of 10.23/12.91 percent and carries a Morningstar rating of two stars. There are a number of additional funds that, while not pure biotech plays, do provide the investor with exposure to firms active in biotechnology. One such fund is the Global Health Sciences closed-end fund. This fund was started in January 1992, carries Morningstar's highest five-star rating and trades at a 25 percent discount to NAV. The fund has one/three-year NAV total returns of 52.04/28.36.

Investing in the Telecommunications Boom

Telecommunication, the ability to place calls where and when we want, is something that people in the United States and the developed nations of Europe have taken for granted for decades. However, for people in the pre-emerging and emerging nations that comprise much of Asia and Latin America, telecommunication as we know it is just a fantasy.

However, as a result of vastly improved economic conditions and more affordable technology, the governments of many lesser developed nations have placed greater emphasis on telecommunications. This new-found hunger for telephone services offers incredible growth potential for those firms that have the knowledge and the wherewithal to meet the challenge.

Funds that concentrate on the telecommunications sector are not rare. Funds with a track record over a year or two are. Presently, there are only a handful of telecommunications funds that have been in existence long enough to achieve a Morningstar rating. Two of these are the Fidelity Select Telecommunications Fund and the G.T. Global Telecommunications Fund. The Fidelity Fund carries the standard Select Fund total load of 3.75 percent, a Morningstar rating of five stars, and five/ten-year total annualized returns of 21.02/18.09 percent. The G.T. Global Fund has not faired quite as well. This Fund has a 4.75 percent front-end load, a Morningstar rating of two stars, and one/three-year total annualized returns of 19.56/13.84 percent.

Investing Abroad

Many investors have heard the case for global diversification. For example, in 1970, the United States accounted for two-thirds of the world-market capitalization. Today, it accounts for about one-third of the total capitalization and its share continues to drop. Also, foreign stocks have outperformed U.S. stocks in every ten-year period ending between 1984 and 1994 except the decade ending in 1984 when the Morgan Stanley Capital International Index (MSCI), the Europe Australia and Far East Index (EAFE), and the S&P 500 Index all had nearly identical returns. Additionally, studies show that adding foreign securities to a domestic portfolio reduces volatility. Finally, since the demise of the Bretton Woods Agreement in 1972 ended the gold standard, the value of the U.S. dollar has declined significantly when compared with hard currency countries.

International funds are not new when compared to some of the sector or trend categories mentioned previously. Consequently, there is a much broader selection from which to choose. However, the cardinal rule of choosing an established fund company with a consistent track record should apply. Two international funds offered by well-known fund families are the Templeton Foreign Fund and the T. Rowe Price International Stock Fund. Templeton Funds were founded by the legendary Sir John Templeton and the fund family enjoys one of the best reputations in the industry. The Foreign Fund is an open-ended fund with 5.75 percent front-end load, a Morningstar rating of four stars, and five/ten-year total annualized returns of 13.10/15.03 percent. T. Rowe Price Investment Services offer a large family of no-load funds. Like Templeton, T. Rowe Price enjoys a solid reputation in the industry. The International Stock Fund carries a Morningstar rating of three stars and five/ten-year total annualized returns of 10.39/14.18 percent.

The Falling Dollar

In the previous section, Investing Abroad, one of the arguments that was made for the global diversification of investment assets was that the value of the U.S. dollar has decreased significantly against many other major currencies. In fact, since 1970, the U.S. dollar has lost more than 75 percent of its value against the strongest world currencies. There are differing opinions on whether this devaluation is the result of our economic situation getting that much worse or whether other nations' economies are getting that much stronger. Regardless, given the state of our trade and current-account deficits, it appears that this trend will likely continue.

One of the best ways to "hedge" against the falling U.S. dollar is to gain exposure to the world's strongest currencies. There is one fund that provides just such an opportunity. The Franklin Templeton Hard Currency Fund normally invests in money-market instruments denominated in the world's strongest currencies, the Swiss franc, the Japanese yen, and the German mark. The fund may also take positions in other currencies from countries with very low inflation rates. This fund is open-ended, has a 3 percent front-end load and a Morningstar rating of one star. The three/five-year total annualized returns are 6.07/8.46 percent.

Investing in Asia

There is a fairly high probability that anyone who has recently purchased an article of clothing, consumer electronics, or a variety of other products, found that the item was manufactured in Southeast Asia. Over the past several decades, the world's manufacturing base has been shifting to this region and the reasons are easy to understand. The governments of many Southeast Asian countries have managed to encourage economic growth while keeping inflation under control. Also, there is a work ethic found among the people of this region that is not duplicated anywhere else in the world. The end result has been astonishing economic growth accompanied by even brighter prospects for the future.

There are a variety of funds, both closed and open-ended, that provide the investor exposure to Southeast Asia. Unfortunately, as was the case with some of the industrial sectors, it is difficult to find funds with established track records. However, one fund that has such a record is the Colonial Newport Tiger Fund. This is an open-end fund with a front-end load of 5.75 percent and a Morningstar rating of four stars. The fund has three/five-year total annualized returns of 17.00/19.10 percent. For the investor that wishes to gain exposure to this region via a closed-end fund, there is the Scudder New Asia Fund. This fund has a Morningstar rating of two stars and trades at a discount to NAV of 8.9 percent. This fund has three/five-year NAV total returns of 8.70/9.17 percent.

Frontier Investing in Pre-Emerging Countries

Pre-emerging countries are the last frontier of the investment world. Pre-emerging nations are those that, due to a combination of economic constraints, technological know-how, education, infrastructure, etc., have not yet attained the status of an emerging market. Due to their pre-emerging status, these nations offer some of the lowest-priced investment assets in the world. However, along with the low multiples comes volatility and risk. Let it suffice to say that investing in pre-emerging nations is not for the faint of heart. However, for those with the stomach for it, markets such as Africa, Russia, Vietnam, and the Czech Republic offer unlimited potential.

There are a number of closed-end country funds that offer the adventurous investor exposure to pre-emerging markets. Most of these funds are relatively new and therefore have little track record to speak of. Also, as a result of their infancy status, most have not yet achieved Morningstar ratings. Four such closed-end funds are the Czech Republic Fund, the Morgan Stanley Africa Investment Fund, the Templeton Russia Fund, and the Templeton Vietnam Opportunities Fund. Three of the four, despite their lack of track record, are offered by well-known and highly regarded fund companies, Morgan Stanley and Templeton. The Czech Republic Fund has a one-year NAV Total return of 29.50 percent and trades at a discount to NAV of 5.3 percent. The Morgan Stanley Africa Investment Fund has a one-year NAV total return of 14.68 percent and trades at a discount to NAV of 21.4 percent. The Templeton Russia Fund has a one-year NAV total return of 61.06 percent and trades at a premium to NAV of 16.6 percent. Finally, the Templeton Vietnam Opportunities Fund has a one-year NAV total return of 5.40 percent and trades at a discount to NAV of 18.8 percent.

Sources

1. Source of ratings and performance information is Morningstar Inc.

2. All open-end fund performance information as of 3/31/96.

3. All closed-end fund performance information as of 6/30/96.

Chapter

14

Building a Portfolio for the 21st Century

Over the past 30 years, portfolio theory has made great strides, as academics have brought this field of finance forward from a loose collection of conventional wisdom and "rule of thumb," and turned it into a science. This new scientific approach to building portfolios is termed *modern portfolio theory*. While it is not our goal here to go into the academic proofs of these theories, we do hope to provide fundamental principles that will be of practical value to you as you build a portfolio for the 21st century.

Principle #1: Market Efficiency

The first principle any investor should remember also applies to all aspects of life—don't expect a free lunch. The fact is markets are "information discounting machines" where buyers and sellers of securities determine the *right* price, satisfactory to both. And what is the right price, you might ask? According to modern theory, the right price is the price that will provide a level of return that is commensurate with the level of market risk associated with the security.

"Wait!" you say. "What about my Amalgamated Widget shares that doubled last year? Isn't that proof against market efficiency? Surely these shares were mispriced at one time or another." Well, market efficiency doesn't promise that all securities at all times are priced to deliver normal returns. It just suggests that on average, and over time, securities deliver returns commensurate with their risks.

Academics have spent years and years looking to prove or disprove the theory of market efficiency, particularly in the United States. On the whole, the evidence suggests that most of the time the U.S. market is efficient (though not perfectly so). One example of this is the fact that more than half of the professionally managed mutual funds in the United States have underperformed the unmanaged market indexes. This suggests that even highly compensated and highly educated professionals have difficulty "beating the market."

The U.S. market is considered the most efficient in the world. The market is large and liquid, information is quickly and widely disseminated, fairly strictly regulated, and insider trading is illegal (though this may actually reduce efficiency). In foreign markets, many or all of these conditions may be absent. Foreign markets can be thin and illiquid, with information hard to come by. Regulations may be lax or nonexistent, and insider trading may be rampant. All these features suggest that foreign markets are less efficient than the U.S. market. This inefficiency can work for you, or against you—inefficiency provides opportunities to find abnormally high returns, or abnormally low returns. Inefficiency places a premium on superior analysis and the proper "connections," both critical elements for above-average investment performance.

Principle #2: Diversification

Suppose that somebody offered you the following scenario: Bet $100,000 on a coin flip, heads you win $250,000, tails you loose your $100,000. The expected return is

$(0.5 \times 0) + (0.5 \times \$250,000) = \$125,000 = 25$ percent

For a person whose net worth is only $100,000, this option may be too risky, even though the return scenario is very much in his or her favor. Consider this contrasting scenario: Bet $10,000 on ten independent coin flips, heads you win $25,000, tails you lose $10,000. The expected return is the same, 25 percent, yet the diversification factor of the second scenario makes the risk much more acceptable.

Similarly, there is the old fable taught to students seeking degrees in finance. Suppose you have an investment portfolio invested in a company that manufactures suntan lotion. While the sun is shining, you will make a lot of money. However, when the rain comes, you tend to lose money. This investment makes your portfolio's performance highly dependent on sunshine. After being soaked, you stumble on a brilliant idea: invest in an umbrella manufacturer! Now, while it's raining, your umbrella stock is rising, thus offsetting the decline in your lotion shares. Continuing with the weather analogy, the investor may then invest in kites for windy days, coats for cold days, etc. Ultimately, the investor is diversified to the point where he or she expects to make decent returns no matter what the weather. This is usually where the traditional lesson on diversification stops. But what has this investor failed to consider? What if now, suntan lotion is increasingly imported from Australia, umbrellas are coming from England, kites are best made in China, and Siberia takes the coat market by storm. Suddenly, the supposedly well-diversified portfolio is crushed by forces outside of the investor's narrow investment universe. True diversification requires a global investment perspective.

Again, diversification can help reduce portfolio risk. Modern portfolio theory teaches us that as one adds more and more individual stocks to a portfolio, eventually company specific risk is diversified away; the ill fortune of one specific company is offset by the good fortune of another. However, one risk that cannot be diversified away is called *systematic* or *market* risk. Market risk is the risk that the security market as a whole delivers to the investor.

We promise not to become too technical here, but there are a few terms that even the casual investor can benefit from understanding. *Beta* is the measure of market risk inherent in a security, and is an indication of the degree that a specific security moves in synch or out of synch with its market. Because U.S. market risk is present in every U.S. stock, it cannot be diversified away by buying more U.S. stocks. This risk is irreducible, and it is this risk that the market pays you for taking. Thus, the return you expect to achieve in the United States is tied to your willingness to assume market or beta risk. For example, in the United States, there are high-flying tech stocks that soar when the market is doing well, and plunge when the market declines. If a specific stock (say, Doubler Electronics Inc.) had a history of rising 20 percent each time the S&P 500 rose 10 percent, and falling 20 percent each time the S&P 500 fell 10 percent, we would say that it had a beta of 2. The market itself always has a beta of 1 (by definition, the market moves exactly in line with itself). Negative beta companies are rare, but possible—some gold stocks have negative or low betas. Consider the following hypothetical negative beta stock: Wall St. Wreckers Inc., specializing in buying failed brokerage firms' electronics equipment to resell as scrap. When the market rises 10 percent, Wall St. Wreckers stock falls 10 percent, and when the market falls 10 percent, Wall St. Wreckers gains 10 percent. This would give it a beta of negative 1. International stocks also have betas. One simply measures a

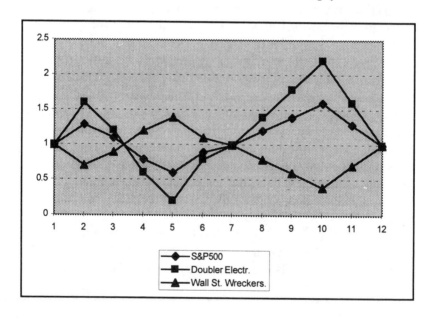

ng

oung, 26, is just starting his career as a software engi-
 large firm. Having a master's degree, Tim is already
$50,000, and expects to make much more as he
. For the first time in his life, he has surplus money to
is many goals: to build up a surplus in case of future
 to supplement his lifestyle, to build a nest egg for a
me purchase, and ultimately, to fund his retirement.
ves that Social Security will probably not be there for
 old age.
as high return expectations, his money will have to
d for him. With a time horizon beyond 20 years, well
21st century, and a high risk tolerance, he is willing to
ort-term fluctuations. Tim doesn't expect to touch his
 for a long time, so Tim will place most of his invest-
an IRA, to defer taxes on his investments.
 factors suggest that Tim should select aggressive
nts. A good mix would include the following:

gn Stocks 45%
50% of foreign stocks in emerging markets)
Stocks 35%
gn Bonds 15%
 or Gold Stocks 5%

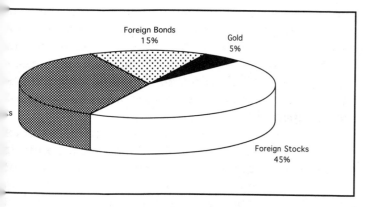

foreign stock versus its local index, just as one measures a U.S. stock versus the S&P 500.

Another important term to understand is *correlation*. It is actually similar to beta, yet it can be applied to a wider array of securities, across national boundaries and between security classes. Correlation measures the extent to which the returns on assets, or asset classes, move in relation to one another. Fortunately for the global investor, all markets do not tend to move in the same direction at the same time and to the same degree. When the U.S. market is falling, other markets may be rising, providing the global investor with wide-scale diversification benefits across markets.

Because of reduced correlation between international markets, the beta, or systematic risk of a foreign stock, is not measuring the same risk as the beta of a U.S. stock in a global portfolio. Adding a high-risk foreign stock may serve to decrease the total portfolio risk of a mostly U.S. portfolio, if the foreign stock is in an uncorrelated market.

In 1974, Bruno Solnik presented a groundbreaking study on the topic of global diversification. He illustrated that as the number of stocks in a portfolio increases, diversification increases, and portfolio risk is reduced. He then showed that the same number of international stocks did an even better job of reducing portfolio risk, as the chart illustrates.

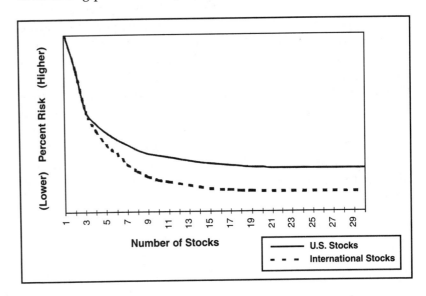

The following chart shows how one can increase the return while reducing the risk of a U.S. stock portfolio by gaining exposure to foreign stock markets (represented by the EAFE Index—Europe, Australia, Far East).

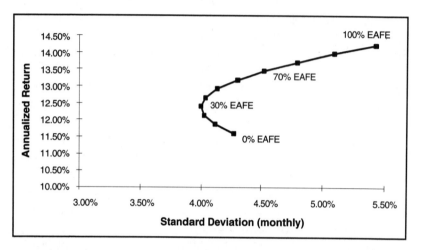

As illustrated in the following table, one can see that though developed foreign markets (EAFE) provided higher returns than the U.S. market (S&P 500), in return for higher volatility. Similarly, international government bonds provided greater returns than lower risk U.S. government bonds. The emerging markets had the highest volatility, with moderate return (albeit measured over a relatively short period of time). Gold has provided almost no return over the past ten years. One may observe in the correlation matrix that the various asset classes shown tend to move independently, suggesting that a mix of these asset classes will increase portfolio diversification. The highest degree of correlation was between the U.S. stock market and the U.S. government bond market, at 50 percent. The lowest correlation was between the U.S. stock market and gold, at –0.31. Gold has exhibited small or negative correlation to other asset classes, providing particularly strong diversification benefits.

	Annualized Return	Historical Volatility	Correlations
S&P 500 (1)	13.97%	14.51%	1
MSII EAFE (1)	15.46%	17.07%	0.434
International Govt. Bond Index (2)	10.73%	10.63%	0.148
U.S. Govt. Bond Index (2)	7.91%	4.44%	0.5
IFC Emerging Mkt. Composite (3)	12.69%	21.77%	0.227
Gold (2)	0.75%	12.38%	-0.312
			S&P 500

(1) = 20-year history Morgan Stanley Capital (Europe, Australia, Far E

(2) = 10-year history International and U.S. Gc by J.P. Morgan

(3) = 5-year history

Through 7/31/96 IFC Emerging Markets C International Finance Co

Principle #3: Invest for A and Return

The best portfolio for the 21st portfolio customized for your situati your risk tolerances. First, define yc return expectations and risk toler returns and risks associated with va future results will almost certainly c historical performances can provide k can be expected.

Then identify your investment cc ity needs, time horizon, tax status, a portfolio must be structured to accom

Here are some examples of how i the portfolio creation process, integra tations with their objectives and cons

Tim Yo

Tim neer for making advance invest. F job loss, future h Tim beli him in h

Tim work ha into the accept s principa ments i

The investm

Fore

U.S.

For

Gol

U.S. Sto 35%

The investments in foreign and U.S. stocks should provide for high returns at a time that Tim can best bear the risk, while a relatively small investment in foreign bonds and gold should provide diversification benefits to the portfolio.

Jack Middleton

Jack Middleton is 48 years old, is married and has two children who have just finished college. He owns a small business, from which he makes a steady income averaging $80,000 a year. Jack plans to pass his business to his children. Currently, he has invested assets of $60,000. Now that his children have finished college, he intends to increase his rate of savings in anticipation of his retirement 20 years from now.

Foreign Stocks 35%
> (33% of foreign stocks in emerging markets)

U.S. Stocks 30%

Foreign Bonds 15%

U.S. Bonds 15%

Gold or Gold Stocks 5%

This portfolio combines the beneficial high returns of equities with the steadying influence of bonds and gold. It represents a good all-round diversified portfolio.

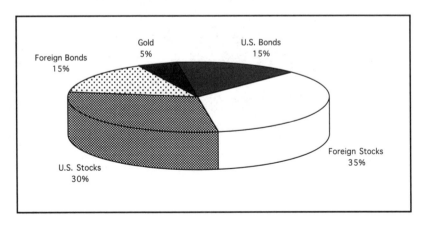

Will Noble

Will Noble is a 67-year-old widower. He recently retired as an engineer from a large aerospace company. He has total investable assets of $300,000, a pension of about $20,000 per year, plus Social Security of $8,000. His house is paid for. He enjoys sailing and traveling in his retirement and requires annual living expenses of $50,000, $22,000 more than his current income. Therefore, Will expects to receive this much income annually from his portfolio, about 7.3 percent of $300,000. He's in generally good health and expects to live another 25 years. Will has many concerns: inflation eating away at the purchasing power of his pension, changes in Social Security removing a secondary source of income, and the fear that someday he may become a burden to his family. He would also like to leave a meaningful inheritance to his children and grandchildren.

U.S. Bonds 40%

Foreign Bonds 30%

U.S. Stocks 15%

Foreign Stocks 10%

Gold or Gold Stocks 5%

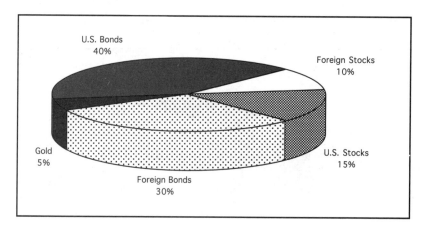

The coupon payments from U.S. and foreign bonds should provide most of Will's income needs, yet the moderate equity exposure and international diversification should help maintain and even grow Will's capital and purchasing power.

Principle #4: Invest Where the Profits Are

Easier said than done, you might say. That's true enough, yet it is an inescapable fact that global trends are changing the world's economies; these trends are identifiable. The changes are powerful enough to deliver riches to investments within some countries and industries, while providing hardship to others. By applying one's reason in an attempt to understand and profit from these changes, one can earn unusually high returns. By "out-thinking" those whose minds are frozen by convention, reflecting on the past rather than anticipating the future, or narrowly focused on their small slice of the world's investment opportunities, an individual investor can be handsomely rewarded.

Traditionally, investors have searched for high profits by examining investments according to two classifications: value and growth. The value investor seeks out unknown or "out of favor" securities with low valuations (suggested by low price-asset, price-earnings, or price-cashflow ratios), hoping that the low valuations are a temporary anomaly that the market will someday wake up to, ultimately pushing up the share price. The growth investor looks primarily at sales and earnings growth, anticipating that a company whose earnings are growing rapidly should deliver share price growth that is unusually high.

While it's good to know today's valuation ratios, and it's helpful to know short-term forecasts for earnings growth, today's ephemeral data are hardly suitable for guiding a portfolio designed for the 21st century. What is needed is the conceptual grasp of the broad economic and investment themes that will provide long-lasting opportunities. Not just a quarterly earnings or economic report, but rather knowledge of the long-term changes sweeping the globe, moving cities and populations from one continent to another, changing the lives of billions.

I've provided you with specific investments that I think will benefit from these trends, specific investments that may be suitable for your 21st century portfolio.

Conclusion

Throughout this book, I have predicted the likelihood—not the inevitability—that certain trends will shape our future. Because trends directly affect the odds of making money in certain investments, they can be friends to investors who are able to read them and play them well. To be successful, an investor must know how to differentiate between fads and trends. Take the hula hoop example I mentioned in the beginning of Chapter 1. The hula hoop was a fad that was part of a larger trend in the plastics industry. Investors who bought into the toy companies that were making hula hoops were investing in a fad and profited only during the hula hoop rage. As for investors who bought into companies in the plastic industry, they were putting their money into a trend and were likely to see profits from their investment long after the hula hoop rage fizzled out.

Picking sound investment vehicles involves more than distinguishing fad from trend. Investors who are motivated by fear and greed in selecting their investments could be duped by industries that rely on these two motivators to persuade them to part with their hard-earned money. For example, in the United States, the insurance industry preys on investors' fears: What happens if a family's only wage earner suddenly disappears? Or a potentially fatal medical emergency occurs? While these events could happen and should be addressed in the investment decision-making process, fear—the emotion driving the decision—should be eliminated. Investors should instead focus on the odds of such calamities happening, whether existing assets can be protected, how future income needs can be calculated now with the assurance that those needs will be met, and most important, is the protection really needed? In effect, a catastrophe or a fear-driven occurrence is the motivator used to enhance existing income.

The stock and bond market are also driven by the emotional motivators fear and greed. In fact, greed is the strongest motivator for the investor who sees an opportunity—based on a tip, a rumor, or media hype—and seizes it without exercising more due diligence, such as seeking more information about price-earnings ratio, growth, earning trends, industry trends, capability of management, and so on. Now that you have read this book, you know how such due diligence enhances your chances of choosing sound and profitable investment vehicles.

I wrote this book as a macroeconomic overview. The trends I discuss are the ones that currently seem to have the most obvious long-term chances for success and durability. Hopefully, the stocks underlying these trends are the ones with the highest profit potential.

Trends change, so to be a successful investor, you must monitor trends carefully—ever alert for old ones fading and new ones emerging. The more you know about the investment process underlying the individual investments, the better you will do.

Two final tips: First, don't focus on only one industry or stock, regardless of how appealing it might be. As long as its value continues to grow, it might merit a home in your portfolio; otherwise, it should be discarded. Second, don't focus on any industry to the extent that you are relying heavily on the performance of a single sector. Diversification—the essence of a good portfolio—will preserve your existing capital and enhance it prudently and conservatively over time.

Good luck as you navigate your investment portfolio through the very exciting global markets of tomorrow.

Appendix

How to Buy and Sell Foreign Stocks and Bonds

Not too long ago, the resources available to the individual investor, for purchasing foreign securities, were quite limited. However, the popularity of the global diversification approach to investing has spawned a variety of options for the purchase of foreign stocks and bonds.

The investor that does not have the time or the expertise to make his own investment decisions may want to enlist the services of a full-service broker/dealer. Within this realm, the investor may wish to choose one of the large *wire-house* firms, such as Merrill Lynch or Prudential Securities. While these large firms offer a variety of services, one must also keep in mind that many are relative newcomers to the world of international investing.

Another option for the client wishing to establish a relationship with a full-service broker would be to choose one of the smaller, "boutique" firms that specializes in global investing. My own firm, International Assets Advisory Corp. (IAAC), is just such a firm. IAAC has been preaching the advantages of global diversification for nearly 15 years, long before global investing became as fashionable as it is today.

For those investors that feel they have the resources and expertise to make their own investment decisions, a discount broker may be the right choice. The universe of discounters has expanded dramatically over the past several years, providing the investor with a wide range of options. However, one must keep in mind that most of these firms offer little in the way of research and many are quite limited in their knowledge of international securities. One notable exception to this generalization is Charles Schwab & Co., Inc. Charles Schwab, the pioneer of the discount brokerage industry, has made a concerted effort to enter the global investing arena through its recently created Guide to Global Investing and global investing services.

Finally, as mentioned in the chapter on mutual funds, there is a virtual plethora of funds available that provide exposure to the global markets. The investor need only choose the type of fund that is best suited to his investment objectives and risk tolerance. Keep in mind the differences between load and no-load funds as well as those of open and closed-end funds.

Regardless of the type of investment vehicle chosen, in this rapidly changing world economy, I believe that it is essential to diversify globally. In addition to the many printed materials available, the Internet and the World Wide Web are an excellent source for researching the global markets, as well as those companies that provide investment products and brokerage services to access those markets.

Index